Holly Jolly Christmas Quilting™

Edited by **JEANNE STAUFFER & SANDRA L. HATCH**

HOUSE of
WHITE
BIRCHES
PUBLISHERS
SINCE 1947

Holly Jolly Christmas Quilting ™

Editors Jeanne Stauffer, Sandra L. Hatch

Art Director Brad Snow

Publishing Services Director Brenda Gallmeyer

Managing Editor Dianne Schmidt

Assistant Art Director Nick Pierce

Copy Supervisor Michelle Beck

Copy Editors Nicki Lehman, Mary O'Donnell

Technical Artist Connie Rand

Graphic Arts Supervisor Ronda Bechinski

Book Design Nick Pierce

Graphic Artist Nicole Gage

Production Assistants Marj Morgan, Judy Neuenschwander

Photography Supervisor Tammy Christian

Photography Don Clark, Matthew Owen

Photo Stylists Tammy M. Smith, Tammy Steiner

Chief Executive Officer David McKee

Book Marketing Director Dwight Seward

Printed in United States of America

First Printing 2007, China

Library of Congress Control Number: 2007921289

Hardcover ISBN: 978-1-59217-184-2

Softcover ISBN: 978-1-59217-185-9

DRGbooks.com

2 3 4 5 6 7 8 9

Have a Holly Jolly Christmas

There's something warm and inviting about the home of a quilter during this festive time of year. It is created by the combination of colors and the whimsical fabrics with holiday motifs. This intangible feeling is contagious—everyone wants it. It doesn't matter whether you are a beginning or more advanced quilter, you'll find the perfect project to set that mood here in this book.

All it takes is a couple of runners, a few pillows, a lap quilt or throw for your sofa and presto!—you have added holiday ambience to a room. Decorate your tree with a quilted tree skirt and some quilted ornaments, and you have a whole new look. Guests will notice that special feeling as soon as they walk into the room. Get ready for requests to reproduce that feeling for family and friends.

After you have completed some of the smaller projects, give your beds a holiday boost by using the patterns provided for several very quick and easy bed-size quilts.

Whether you quilt to decorate your home for the holidays or to make gifts for family and friends, we know you will enjoy the patterns created by our designers especially for you. When the holidays are over, many of these patterns can be made for any time of the year by selecting different fabrics in a variety of color combinations that coordinate with your home decor.

No matter how you use the patterns in this book, we know they will enrich your holidays. We hope you have a Holly Jolly Christmas and great fun quilting the whole year through.

Jeanne Stauffer

Sandra L. Hatch

Contents

Joy Snowman

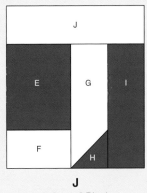
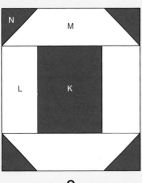
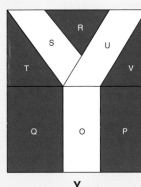

Design by **CONNIE KAUFFMAN**

Paper-pieced Snowball blocks are the perfect designs for this cute little banner.

J
3¾" x 4¼" Block

O
3¾" x 4¼" Block

Y
3¾" x 4¼" Block

Large Snowball
2¾" x 2¾" Block

Small Snowball
2¼" x 2¼" Block

PROJECT SPECIFICATIONS

Skill Level: Intermediate

Quilt Size: 16" x 18" (without tabs)

Block Size: 2¼" x 2¼", 2¾" x 2¾" and 3¾" x 4¼"

Number of Blocks: 1 each pattern

MATERIALS

- Scraps orange and brown
- ¼ yard white silver metallic
- ⅜ yard blue snowflake print
- Backing 18" x 20"
- Batting 18" x 20"
- All-purpose thread to match fabrics
- Quilting thread
- 4" x 5" scrap fusible web
- 2 black E beads
- 3 clear E beads
- 4 blue seed beads
- 10 (⅝") snowflake buttons
- 1 (1⅛") snowflake
- Black, fine-point permanent fabric marker
- Basic sewing tools and supplies

CUTTING

Step 1. Cut one of each of the following pieces from white silver metallic: 3½" x 3½" A, 3 x 3" C, 2½" x 16½" AA, 4" x 18⅜" BB, 1¾" x 2½" F, 1¾" x 4" G, 1¾" x 4½" J, 1¾" x 3" O, 1½" x 3½" S and 1½" x 4" U.

Step 2. Cut two of each of the following pieces from white silver metallic: 1¾" x 3" L and 1¾" x 4½" M.

Step 3. Cut one of each of the following pieces from blue snowflake print: 2½" x 3" E, 1¾" x 1¾" H, 1¾" x 4" I, 2½" x 3" K, 2" x 3" P, 2¼" x 3" Q, 2½" x 2½" R, 2½" x 2¾" T, 2" x 3" V and 3¾" x 16½" Y.

Step 4. Cut two of each of the following pieces from blue snowflake print: 2⅞" x 4¾" Z, 3¼" x 7⅛" W and 2¾" x 7⅜" X.

Step 5. Cut the following from blue snowflake print: four 1¾" x 1¾" N, four 2½" x 6½" CC and eight 1½" x 1½" B/D.

Step 6. Trace one nose and two arm shapes onto the paper side of the fusible web; cut out shapes, leaving a margin around each one.

Step 7. Fuse paper shapes on the wrong side of the scraps as directed on patterns for color; cut out shapes on traced lines. Remove paper backing.

COMPLETING THE BLOCKS

Step 1. Prepare one copy of each of the paper-piecing patterns.

Step 2. Shorten the stitch length on your machine to 18–20 stitches per inch.

Step 3. Beginning with the J pattern, place fabric to cover area E on the paper pattern with wrong side of fabric against the unmarked side of the paper.

Step 4. Place fabric for area F right sides together with fabric E on the E-F edge as shown in Figure 1; pin along the E-F line. Fold fabric F over to cover area F as shown in Figure 2, allowing fabric to extend at least ¼" into adjacent areas as shown in Figure 3; adjust fabric if necessary. Unfold fabric F to lie flat on fabric E.

Figure 1   **Figure 2**   **Figure 3**

Step 5. Flip paper pattern; stitch on the E-F line, beginning and ending 2 or 3 stitches into adjacent areas as shown in Figure 4. Stitch to (or beyond) the outside heavy solid line on outer edges as shown in Figure 5.

Figure 4   **Figure 5**

Step 6. Trim the E-F seam allowance to ⅛"–¼" as shown in Figure 6. Fold fabric F to cover area F; lightly press with a warm dry iron.

Figure 6

Step 7. Continue to add fabrics in alphabetical order to cover the paper pattern as shown in Figure 7. Check that each piece will cover its area before stitching.

Figure 7   **Figure 8**

Step 8. Pin outside fabric edges to the paper pattern. Trim paper and fabric edges even on the outside heavy solid line as shown in Figure 8.

Step 9. Repeat Steps 1–8 to complete one of each block.

COMPLETING THE BANNER

Step 1. Join the J, O and Y blocks with two Z pieces to make the Z row as shown in Figure 9; press seams toward Z strips and toward the O block.

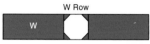

Figure 9

Step 2. Sew the Large Snowball block between two W strips to complete the W row as shown in Figure 10; press seams toward W strips.

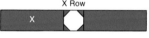

Figure 10

Step 3. Sew a Small Snowball block between two X strips to make an X row as shown in Figure 11; press seams toward X strips.

Figure 11

Step 4. Join the pieced rows with the AA and Y strips referring to the Placement Diagram for positioning of rows and strips; press seams in one direction.

Step 5. Remove paper backing from each paper-pieced block.

Step 6. Fold the BB strip in half and cut from corner to corner to make a BB triangle as shown in Figure 12.

Figure 12

Step 7. Sew the BB triangle to the AA end of the pieced top; press seam toward AA.

Step 8. Arrange the nose and arm shapes on the pieced top referring to the Placement Diagram and project photo for placement; fuse in place. Using thread to match, machine satin-stitch around the nose shape.

Joy Snowman
Placement Diagram
16" x 18"
(without tabs)

Step 9. Add a smile to the Small Snowball block using the black, fine-point permanent fabric marker referring to the Placement Diagram and project photo for suggestions.

Step 10. Fold each CC strip in half along length with right sides together; stitch along the length to make a tube as shown in Figure 13; turn right side out and press with seam on the edge to complete one hanging tab. Repeat to make four hanging tabs.

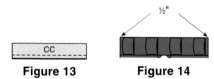

Figure 13   **Figure 14**

Step 11. Pin one tab ½" from each end of the Y edge of the pieced top referring to Figure 14; pin the remaining hanging tabs equally spaced between the end tabs. Machine-baste ⅛" from edge to hold.

Step 12. Lay the pieced top right sides together with the backing and place on the batting on a flat surface; pin or baste edges together to hold flat. Stitch all around, leaving a 4" opening on one side.

Step 13. Clip corners; trim batting close to seam. Turn right side out through opening, poking out corners and smoothing edges at seam; press.

Step 14. Fold seam allowance at the opening to the inside; press. Hand-stitch opening closed.

Step 15. Quilt as desired by hand or machine.

Step 16. Add the ⅝" snowflake buttons to the blue snowflake print areas. Sew black beads to the Small Snowball block for eyes.

Step 17. String blue and clear beads on a thread and sew the 1⅛" snowflake to the end to make a small tassle. Sew to the bottom point of the quilt to finish. ❖

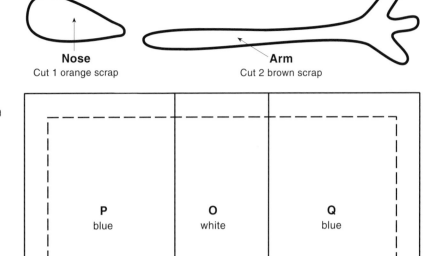

Nose
Cut 1 orange scrap

Arm
Cut 2 brown scrap

Y Bottom Paper-Piecing Pattern

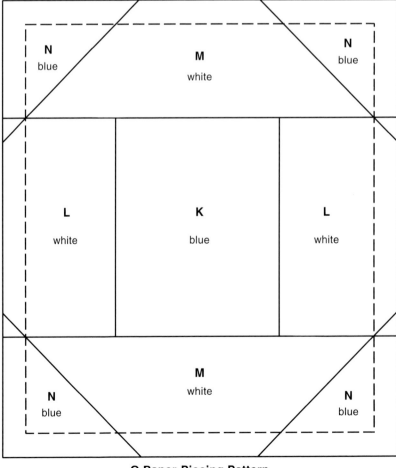

O Paper-Piecing Pattern

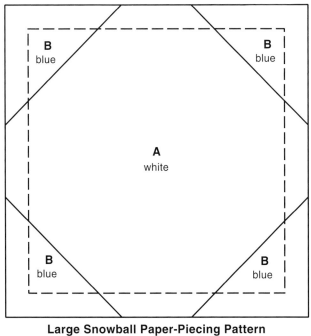

Large Snowball Paper-Piecing Pattern

Small Snowball Paper-Piecing Pattern

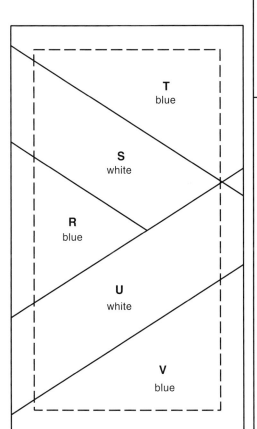

Y Top Paper-Piecing Pattern

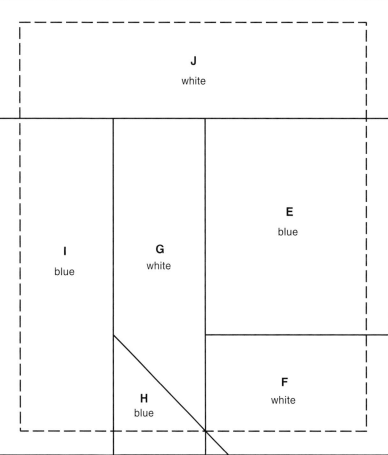

J Paper-Piecing Pattern

Waiting for Santa

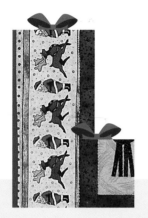

Design by **CONNIE RAND**

Santa's reindeer are ready, but he's still busy packing up his sleigh!

PROJECT NOTE

The border stripe used in the sample ran across the width of the fabric from selvage to selvage. If your stripe runs along the length of the fabric, you will need to purchase 1 yard and cut the D and E border along the length.

PROJECT SPECIFICATIONS

Skill Level: Beginner
Quilt Size: 32" x 15"

MATERIALS

- Scraps of 1 tan and 2 brown tonals
- ¼ yard gold tonal
- ¼ yard red print
- ¼ yard red solid
- ⅓ yard Christmas stripe
- Backing 38" x 21"
- Batting 38" x 21"
- All-purpose thread to match fabrics
- Quilting thread
- ¼ yard fusible web
- 8 (7mm) googly eyes
- Fabric glue
- Water-erasable marker
- Basic sewing tools and supplies

CUTTING

Step 1. Cut one 7½" x 24½" A rectangle gold tonal.

Step 2. Cut two 1½" x 24½" B strips and two 1½" x 9½" C strips red print.

Step 3. Cut four 3½" x 3½" F squares red print.

Step 4. Cut two 3½" x 9½" D strips and two 3½" x 26½" E strips Christmas stripe.

Step 5. Cut three 2¼" by fabric width strips red solid for binding.

COMPLETING THE QUILT

Step 1. Trace reindeer patterns on paper side of fusible web, referring to patterns for number to cut and leaving a space between each piece. Cut out shapes, leaving a margin around each piece.

Step 2. Fuse shapes to wrong side of tan and brown tonals as directed with patterns. Cut shapes on marked lines; remove paper backing.

Step 3. Draw a line 1" from one long side of the A rectangle, using the water-erasable marker.

Step 4. Arrange reindeer on the background on the drawn line referring to Placement Diagram and photo for positioning. Fuse in place according to manufacturer's directions.

Note: Arrange the legs of the Side-Facing Reindeer in different positions.

Step 5. Sew B strips to the top and bottom and C strips to opposite sides of the pieced center; press seams toward the B and C strips.

Step 6. Sew D strips to opposite sides of the pieced center; press seams toward D strips.

Step 7. Sew an F square to each end of each E strip; press seams toward E strips.

Step 8. Sew the E-F strips to the top and bottom of the pieced center; press seams toward the E-F strips.

Step 9. Layer the batting between the completed top and prepared backing piece; baste, pin or spray-baste to hold.

Step 10. Using brown all-purpose thread, machine-stitch close to edges of all appliqué pieces to hold in place.

Step 11. Quilt and bind referring to Completing Your Quilt on page 173.

Step 12. Glue a googly eye on each reindeer to finish. ❖

WAITING FOR SANTA

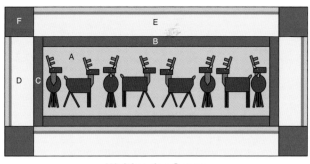

Waiting for Santa
Placement Diagram
32" x 15"

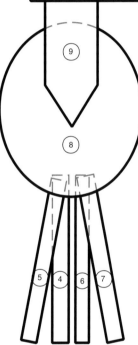

Front-Facing Reindeer
Make 2 (reverse 1)
Cut pieces 1–3 & 9 from brown tonal 1,
pieces 4–8 & 10 from brown tonal 2 &
piece 11 from tan tonal.

Side-Facing Reindeer
Make 4 (reverse 2)
Cut pieces 1–4 & from
brown tonal 1, pieces
5–10 from brown tonal
2 & piece 12 from
tan tonal.

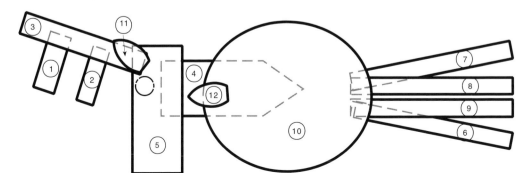

Rear-Facing Reindeer
Make 2 (reverse 1)
Cut pieces 1–4 from brown tonal 1, pieces 5–10 from brown tonal 2 & pieces 11 & 12 from tan tonal.

Flying Santas Tree Skirt

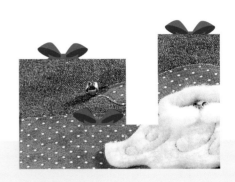

Design by **CHRIS MALONE**

Appliquéd Santas fly around the outside edge of this denim tree skirt.

PROJECT SPECIFICATIONS
Skill Level: Beginner
Tree Skirt Size: 44" diameter (without fringe)

MATERIALS
- Scraps 8 assorted red prints
- Scraps 8 assorted gold prints
- Scraps black and peach solids
- 9" x 12" rectangle each white and cream plush felt
- 2⅝ yards denim
- Batting 50" x 50"
- All-purpose thread to match fabrics
- Black embroidery floss or pearl cotton
- 1 yard fusible web
- 16 (3mm) black beads
- 8 (5mm) red beads
- 8 (⅜") brass bells
- 8 (½") black buttons
- 2 yards ⅞"-wide blue grosgrain ribbon
- 4 yards red large ball fringe

- Cosmetic powder blush and cotton-tip swab
- Double sheet newspaper, pencil and string to make paper pattern
- White marking pencil
- Embroidery needle
- Fabric glue
- No-fray solution
- Basic sewing tools and supplies

CUTTING
Step 1. Fold newspaper in quarters.
Note: The paper should be at least 45" square.
Step 2. Tie one end of the string to a pencil and measure 22¼" from the tied end.
Step 3. Hold the 22¼" point at the folded corner of the paper and swing the pencil from one edge of the paper to the other edge, marking a quarter-circle on the paper as shown in Figure 1.

19¼"

22¼"

3"

Figure 1

Step 4. Repeat Step 3 with the string only 3" long to mark the inner circle, again referring to Figure 1.

Step 5. Cut out the paper on the marked line. *Note: The skirt should measure 19¼" between the bottom edge and the center opening, again referring to Figure 1.*

Step 6. Cut a straight line from the inner circle to the outer edge for the skirt opening in the back.

Step 7. Cut one denim piece each for front and backing using the newspaper pattern.

Step 8. Trace eight each Santa suit, hat, boot, mitten, face and star appliqué shapes onto the paper side of the fusible web using patterns given. Cut out shapes, leaving a margin around each one.

Step 9. Fuse paper shapes to the wrong side of fabric scraps as directed on patterns for color.

Step 10. Cut out shapes on traced lines; remove paper backing.

Step 11. Using patterns given, cut eight each hat, suit and sleeve trim from antique cream plush felt and eight each beard and mustache shapes from white plush felt.

COMPLETING THE APPLIQUÉ

Step 1. Arrange and fuse the appliqué shapes (except plush felt pieces) on the front piece in numerical order with boot of one Santa 4" from one back opening edge and body about 3⅛" up from the bottom edge of the skirt referring to Figure 2 and the Placement Diagram. *Note: Evenly space each Santa motif around the skirt; there will be about 4¼" between the mitten of one Santa and the boot of the next Santa. Do not add star shapes at this point.*

Figure 2

Step 2. Transfer the lines for the star trails to the front piece with the white marking pencil.

Step 3. Using the embroidery needle and black embroidery floss or pearl cotton, outline-stitch on the marked line.

Step 4. Arrange and fuse a star shape at the end of each trail.

Step 5. Using thread to match fabrics, straight-stitch close to the edge of each fused shape.

Step 6. Transfer the curl lines to the wrong side of each beard shape; stitch on the marked lines using black thread.

Step 7. Use fabric glue to secure the beard and sleeve, suit and hat trim plush felt pieces to the Santa motifs.

Step 8. Apply powder blush to the face shapes to make cheeks using a cotton-tip swab.

Step 9. To make mustaches, sew a small gathering stitch down the center of each plush felt mustache shape and pull to gather mustache in the center.

Step 10. Apply fabric glue only in the center of the mustache pieces and secure on the Santa motifs. The ends will be loose.

Step 11. Sew the black beads to the faces for eyes and a red bead above the mustaches for noses.

COMPLETING THE TREE SKIRT

Step 1. Cut the grosgrain ribbon into four 18" lengths.

Step 2. Pin one end of two pieces ⅜" down from the inside open edge as shown in Figure 3; baste to hold in place.

Step 3. Pin one end of each of the two remaining pieces 9" from the inside open edge, again referring to Figure 3; baste to hold in place.

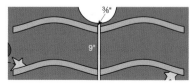

Figure 3

Step 4. Cut a V notch in the end of each piece of ribbon as shown in Figure 4; apply no-fray solution.

Figure 4

Step 5. Layer and pin the appliquéd front piece right sides together with the backing piece; sew all around, leaving a 6" opening along one straight edge of the opening.

Step 6. Clip curves, trim corners and turn right side out through opening; press.

Step 7. Fold the opening seam allowance in ¼" and press. Hand-stitch opening closed.

Step 8. Topstitch ¼" from edges all around.

Step 9. Sew a black button to the center of each star and a bell to the end of each hat, sewing through all layers.

Step 10. Apply no-fray solution to one end of the ball fringe; let dry.

Step 11. Carefully glue the ball fringe around the bottom edge of the tree skirt, gluing one section at a time. When you reach the end, trim fringe to fit and apply no-fray solution to the cut end. When dry, glue the end in place to finish. ❖

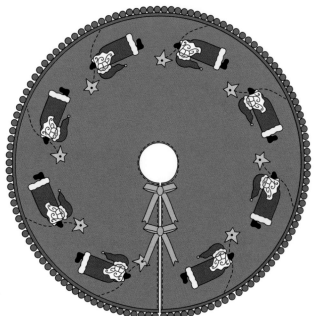

Flying Santas Tree Skirt
Placement Diagram
44" Diameter
(without fringe)

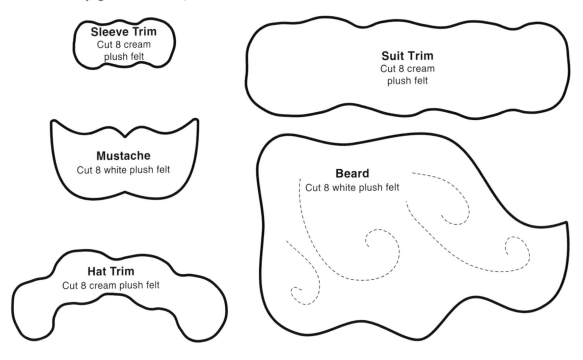

Sleeve Trim
Cut 8 cream
plush felt

Suit Trim
Cut 8 cream
plush felt

Mustache
Cut 8 white plush felt

Beard
Cut 8 white plush felt

Hat Trim
Cut 8 cream plush felt

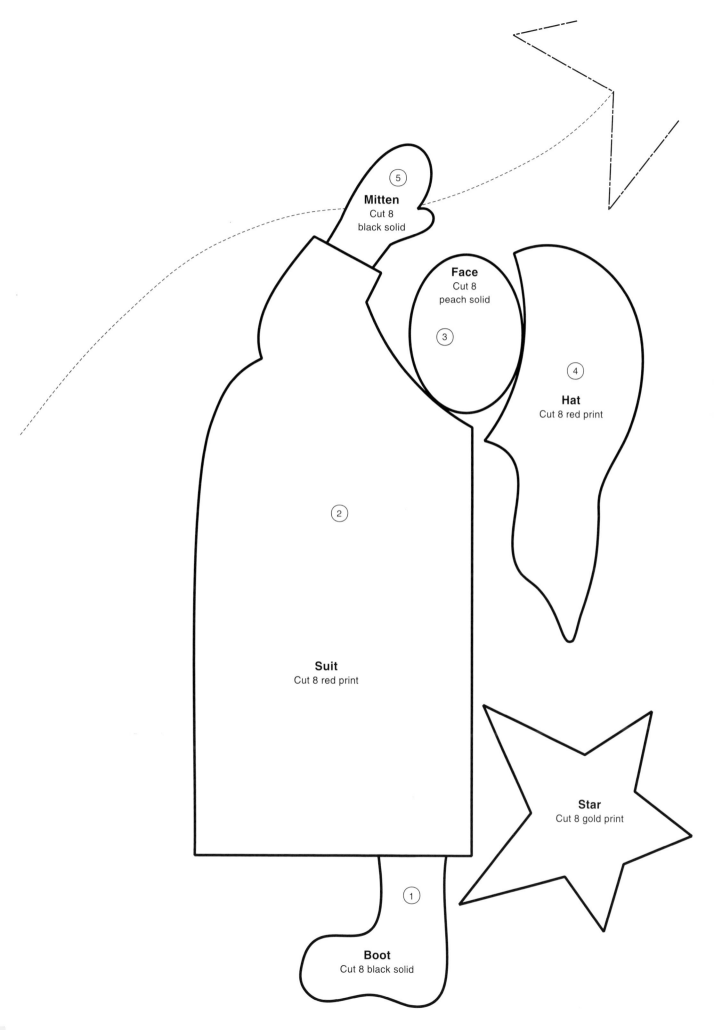

Mitten
Cut 8
black solid
⑤

Face
Cut 8
peach solid
③

Hat
Cut 8 red print
④

Suit
Cut 8 red print
②

Star
Cut 8 gold print

Boot
Cut 8 black solid
①

Jolly Christmas Stocking

Design by **CHRISTINE SCHULTZ**

A variety of Seminole strips decorate the top of Christmas stockings.

PROJECT SPECIFICATIONS
Skill Level: Intermediate
Stocking Size: 10½" x 16½"

MATERIALS
For the cream version:
- 1 fat quarter each cream and red prints
- ⅔ yard green print
- ½ yard muslin or lining fabric

For the blue version:
- 1 fat quarter each white, red, blue and green tonals
- ½ yard blue snowman print
- ½ yard muslin or lining fabric

For both versions:
- All-purpose thread to match fabrics
- Basic sewing tools and supplies

CUTTING
Note: *The instructions are given for the blue version with the cream version in parentheses. Cut strips from the 18" side of the fat quarters.*

Carefully label all strips with the assigned letters.

Step 1. Cut two 18"-long strips in each of the following widths from white tonal (cream print): 1¾" A; 1½" C; 1¼" F and 2½" N.

Step 2. Cut one each 1½" x 18" I, P and R strips white tonal (cream print).

Step 3. Cut two 2" x 18" L strips and one 1½" x 18" LL strip white tonal (cream print).

Step 4. Cut one 18"-long strip in each of the following widths from green tonal: 1" B (red print); 1" H (red print) and 2" K (green print).

Step 5. Cut two 18"-long strips in each of the following widths from green tonal: ¾" D (red print) and 1" M (green print).

Step 6. Cut one 18"-long strip in each of the following widths from blue tonal (green print): 1" E and 1½" S.

Step 7. Cut two 1" x 18" G strips blue tonal (green print).

Step 8. Cut one 18"-long strip in each of the following widths from red tonal (red print): 2" J, ¾" O and 1½" Q.

Step 9. Cut stocking pieces as directed using patterns given.

Step 10. Prepare 60" of 2¼"-wide bias binding from blue snowman print (green tonal).

COMPLETING BAND 1

Step 1. Sew a B strip between two A strips with right sides together along the length to make an A-B strip set; press seams toward B.

Step 2. Subcut the A-B strip set into two ¾" A-B units as shown in Figure 1.

Figure 1   Figure 2

Step 3. Sew C to D to E to D to C with right sides together along the length to make a C-D-E strip set; press seams toward D.

Step 4. Subcut the C-D-E strip set into six 1¼" C-D-E units as shown in Figure 2.

Step 5. Sew F to G to H to G to F with right sides together along the length to make an F-G-H strip set; press seams toward H.

Step 6. Subcut the F-G-H strip set into three 1¼" F-G-H units as shown in Figure 3.

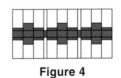

Figure 3   Figure 4

Step 7. To make band 1, join the strip sets made in Steps 1–6 as shown in Figure 4; press seams in one direction.

COMPLETING BAND 2

Step 1. Sew J to I to K with right sides together along the length to make a J-I-K strip set; press seams away from I.

Step 2. Subcut the J-I-K strip set into seven 1½" J-I-K units as shown in Figure 5.

Step 3. Join the units, reversing every other one as shown in Figure 6; press seams in one direction.

Figure 5   Figure 6

Step 4. Trim each long edge of the strip ¼" from the corners of the I squares and trim each end to yield a 7¾"-long strip as shown in Figure 7 to complete band 2.

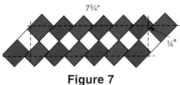

Figure 7

COMPLETING BAND 3

Step 1. Sew L to M to LL to M to L with right sides together along the length to make an L-M strip set; press seams toward M.

Step 2. Subcut the L-M strip set into (10) 1" L-M units as shown in Figure 8.

Figure 8

Step 3. Sew an O strip between two N strips with right sides together along the length to make an N-O strip set; press seams toward N.

Step 4. Subcut the N-O strip set into (10) ¾" N-O units as shown in Figure 9.

Figure 9

Step 5. Join the L-M and N-O units, alternating and offsetting them as shown in Figure 10; press seams in one direction.

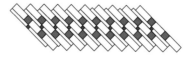

Figure 10

Step 6. Center the pattern formed with M and O pieces and trim strip to 3" x 7¾" as shown in Figure 11 to complete band 3.

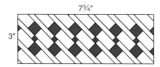

Figure 11

COMPLETING BAND 4

Step 1. Sew the P strip to the Q strip with right sides together along the length to make a P-Q strip set; press seam toward Q. Repeat with R and S strips; press seam toward S.

Step 2. Subcut the P-Q and R-S strip sets into six 1½" P-Q and seven R-S units as shown in Figure 12.

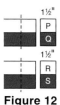 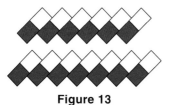

Figure 12   **Figure 13**

Step 3. Join the P-Q units to make a strip as shown in Figure 13; press seams in one direction. Repeat with the R-S strips.

Step 4. Trim the Q and S sides of the strips ¼" from the P and R corners as shown in Figure 14.

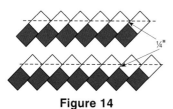

Figure 14

Step 5. Join the trimmed P-Q and R-S strips as shown in Figure 15; press seams toward the P-Q strip.

Figure 15

Blue Jolly Christmas Stocking
Placement Diagram
10½" x 16½"

Traditional Jolly Christmas Stocking
Placement Diagram
10½" x 16½"

Step 6. Trim the long edges of the strip ¼" from the P and R corners and trim the ends to yield a 7¾"-long strip as shown in Figure 16 to complete band 4.

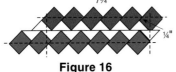

Figure 16

COMPLETING THE STOCKING

Step 1. Join the pieced bands as shown in Figure 17 to complete the pieced top of the stocking; press seams in one direction.

Figure 17

Step 2. Sew the pieced stocking top section to the matching fabric toe/heel piece to complete the stocking front; press seam toward toe piece.

Step 3. Use the stocking front piece to cut one each lining and reverse lining pieces and a reverse backing piece from blue snowman print (green print).

Step 4. Match lining pieces with stocking pieces with right sides together; stitch across the top edge as shown in Figure 18.

Figure 18

Step 5. Turn lining to the wrong side and press top edge.

Step 6. Lay the stitched front and back pieces with lining sides together, matching raw edges; pin or baste layers together around raw edges to hold.

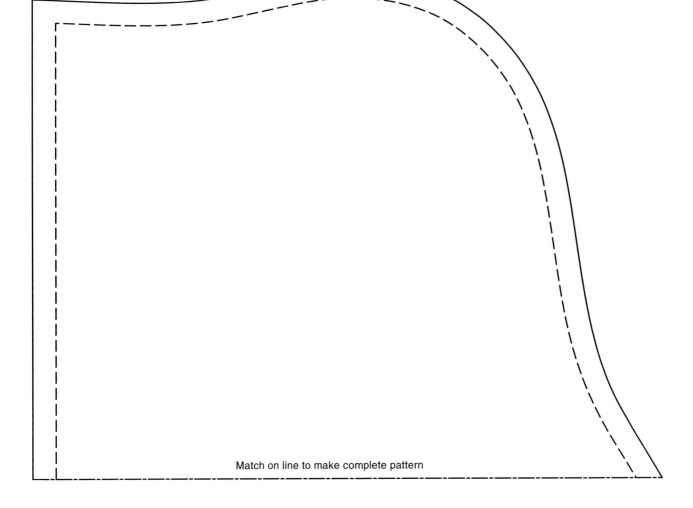

Match on line to make complete pattern

Step 7. Fold bias binding strip with wrong sides together along the length; press.

Step 8. Turn under one end of the binding strip ¼". Pin the folded end of the binding to the top toe edge of the stocking, matching raw edges.

Step 9. Stitch the binding all around, leaving an 8" tail on the heel side. Fold the tail in half along length and stitch edge closed; place the end of the tail on the binding seam on the stocking back 1¼" from top edge as shown in Figure 19; stitch in place.

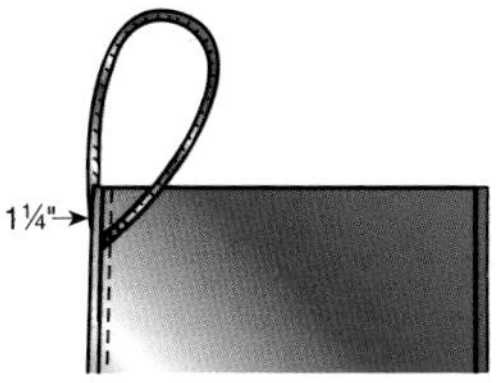

1¼"→

Figure 19

Step 10. Press binding flat on the right side; turn to the stocking back and hand-stitch in place to finish. ❖

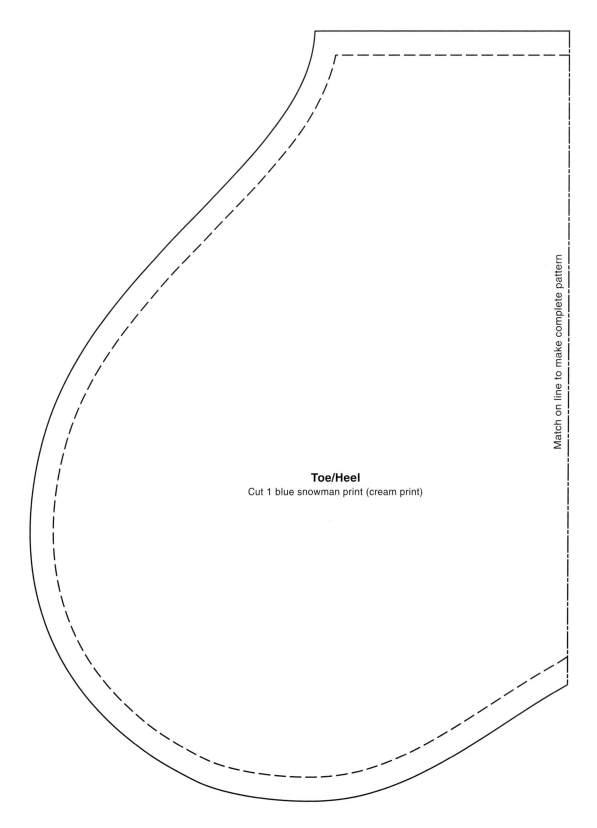

Toe/Heel
Cut 1 blue snowman print (cream print)

Match on line to make complete pattern

Holiday Towel Drapes

Design by **CONNIE KAUFFMAN**

Dress up your towels during the holiday season with a simple little towel drape.

PROJECT SPECIFICATIONS
Skill Level: Beginner
Drape Size: 3" x 17¾"

Christmas Tree Towel Drape
MATERIALS
- Scraps green tonal and brown mottled
- ⅛ yard or 1 fat quarter red print
- 4" x 18" scrap thin batting
- All-purpose thread to match fabrics
- 1 gold star button
- 11 gold seed beads
- 4" x 6" rectangle fusible web
- Basic sewing tools and supplies

Jingle Bell Towel Drape
MATERIALS
- Scrap gold tonal
- ⅛ yard or 1 fat quarter green tonal
- 4" x 18" scrap thin batting

- All-purpose thread to match fabrics
- 20" (⅛"-wide) red satin ribbon
- 3" x 5" rectangle fusible web
- Basic sewing tools and supplies

Christmas Gift Towel Drape
MATERIALS
- Scrap red mottled
- ⅛ yard or 1 fat quarter green print
- 4" x 18" scrap thin batting
- All-purpose thread to match fabrics
- 20" (¼"-wide) white satin ribbon
- 1½" x 4" rectangle fusible web
- Basic sewing tools and supplies

Mitten Towel Drape
MATERIALS
- Scraps lavender mottled and lavender print
- ⅛ yard or 1 fat quarter cream print
- 4" x 18" scrap thin batting

- All-purpose thread to match fabrics
- Invisible thread
- 24" decorative thread or yarn
- 3" x 3" square fusible web
- Basic sewing tools and supplies

Star Towel Drape

MATERIALS

- Scrap white solid
- ⅛ yard or 1 fat quarter blue print
- 4" x 18" scrap thin batting
- All-purpose thread to match fabrics
- Silver metallic thread
- 8 (¼"-long) silver bugle beads
- 1 large sequin
- 1 (⅛") round clear/silver bead
- 3" x 4" rectangle fusible web
- Basic sewing tools and supplies

COMPLETING THE TOWEL DRAPES

Note: The cutting and assembly are the same for each towel drape.

Step 1. Cut two strips 3½" x 18¼" from the ⅛ yard or fat quarter.

Step 2. Fold the corners of one of the pieces to the center and crease as shown in Figure 1.

Figure 1   **Figure 2**

Step 3. Unfold the fabric and cut on the creased lines as shown in Figure 2. Repeat on each end of both strips.

Step 4. Referring to the Placement Diagrams and appliqué shapes given for each towel drape, trace shapes onto the paper side of the fusible web using patterns given.

Step 5. Cut out shapes, leaving a margin around each one.

Step 6. Fuse shapes to the wrong side of fabric scraps as directed on patterns for color; cut out shapes on traced lines. Remove paper backing.

Step 7. Arrange and fuse the appliqué motifs at one end of one of the trimmed pieces referring to the individual Placement Diagrams and specific instructions for each project that follow for positioning.

Step 8. Using thread to match fabrics and a very narrow close zigzag stitch, sew around the edges of each fused shape.

Step 9. After appliqués and embellishments have been added, layer the batting, backing right side up and completed top piece right side down; sew all around, leaving a 3" opening on one side.

Step 10. Trim batting close to stitching; trim the points.

Step 11. Turn right side out; press.

Step 12. Turn opening seam to the inside; hand-stitch opening closed.

Step 13. Quilt as desired around appliqués and embellishments to finish. *Note: When draping over towels, if end seems to pop out, sew a piece of hook tape to the end so it will stick to the towel.*

CHRISTMAS TREE TOWEL DRAPE

Step 1. Center the trunk shape 1½" from the bottom point and fuse in place.

Step 2. Center, fuse and appliqué tree shape over trunk.

Step 3. Stitch around the fused shape using thread to match the towel drape fabric.

Step 4. Sew the star button to the top and the gold seed beads on the tree to finish.

JINGLE BELL TOWEL DRAPE

Step 1. Leave the top edge of each bell unfused until after ribbon is added.

Step 2. To add ribbon, position the ribbon ends into the unfused openings in the bells and finish fusing as shown in Figure 3.

Figure 3

Step 3. Arrange the ribbon

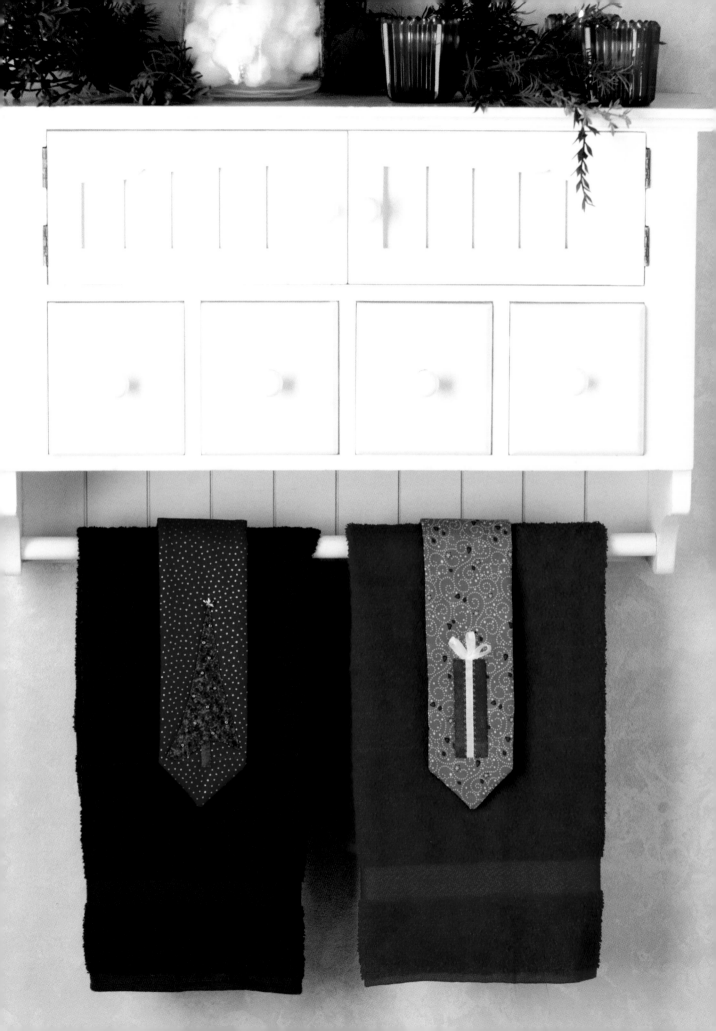

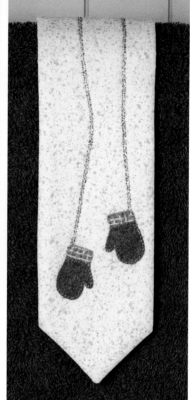

referring to the Placement Diagram; stitch down on each side using thread to match the ribbon.

Step 4. When towel drape base is finished, stitch close to the edges of the bells and ribbon pieces using thread to match towel drape.

CHRISTMAS GIFT TOWEL DRAPE

Step 1. Cut a 3¼" length of the ¼"-wide white ribbon.

Step 2. Center and baste in place on the gift appliqué; fold under excess at each end.

Step 3. Center and fuse the bottom of the gift shape in place, stopping ¾" from the top edge.

Step 4. Make three loops with the remainder of the ribbon and tack ends together as shown in Figure 4.

Figure 4

Step 5. Place the ends of the loops under the top edge of the gift and complete fusing.

Step 6. Complete stitching gift in place and close gift edges to finish.

MITTEN TOWEL DRAPE

Step 1. Arrange the mitten pieces on the towel drape.

Step 2. Before fusing, place the ends of the 24" decorative thread or yarn under the top edge

of each mitten as shown in Figure 5; stitch the thread or yarn in place using invisible thread.

Figure 5

Step 3. Fuse the mitten shapes in place and stitch around the edge to finish.

STAR TOWEL DRAPE

Step 1. Stitch around the appliqué shapes with silver metallic thread and in an X through the center of the star as shown in Figure 6.

Figure 6

Step 2. Sew the bugle beads along the sewn X.

Step 3. Sew the sequin and round bead to the center between the points. ❖

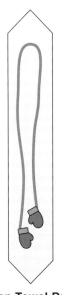

Christmas Tree Towel Drape
Placement Diagram
3" x 17¾"

Jingle Bell Towel Drape
Placement Diagram
3" x 17¾"

Christmas Gift Towel Drape
Placement Diagram
3" x 17¾"

Mitten Towel Drape
Placement Diagram
3" x 17¾"

Star Towel Drape
Placement Diagram
3" x 17¾"

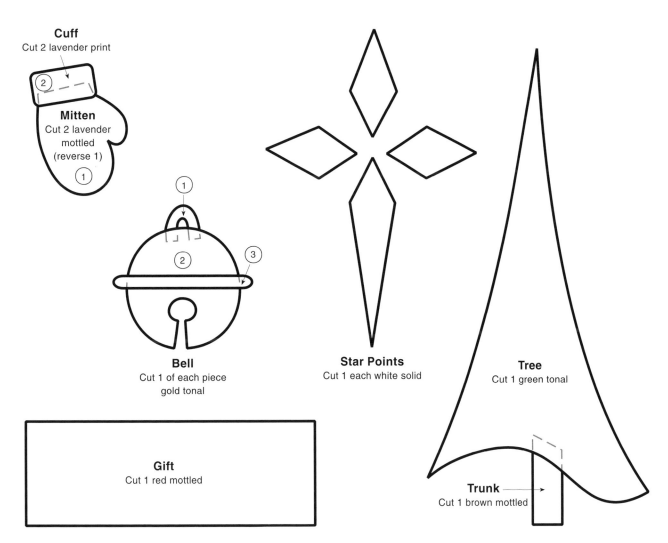

Cuff
Cut 2 lavender print

2

Mitten
Cut 2 lavender mottled
(reverse 1)

1

1

2

3

Bell
Cut 1 of each piece
gold tonal

Star Points
Cut 1 each white solid

Tree
Cut 1 green tonal

Gift
Cut 1 red mottled

Trunk
Cut 1 brown mottled

Holly Jolly Ornaments

Design by **CHRIS MALONE**

Add something special to any Christmas tree.

Angel With Bell
PROJECT SPECIFICATIONS
Skill Level: Intermediate
Ornament Size: 6½" high

MATERIALS
- Scraps light green tonal and pale pink solid
- ⅛ yard white tonal
- Scraps fleece or needled polyester batting
- All-purpose thread to match fabrics
- 1½"-diameter wooden disc or rounded button
- 1 yard ⅝" red satin ribbon (wire-edge optional)
- 2 (³⁄₁₆") black buttons
- 1 (¾") white button
- 9 (6mm) red beads
- Red beading or quilting thread
- ⅞" silver jingle bell
- 4" length ⅝"-wide silver ribbon
- 8" length silver cord
- Cosmetic blush and cotton-tip swab
- Fabric glue
- Large-eye embroidery needle
- Basic sewing tools and supplies

COMPLETING THE ORNAMENT
Step 1. Trace angel body and arm pieces onto the wrong side of the white tonal, reversing pattern for second arm.

Step 2. Fold fabric in half with drawn lines on top and pin to a scrap of fleece or needled batting.

Step 3. Sew all around traced shapes, leaving top edge open on body; repeat on layered arm pieces, leaving no opening.

Step 4. Cut out each shape ⅛" from seam; clip curves.

Step 5. Turn body shape right side out through top opening; press.

Step 6. Machine- or hand-stitch top opening closed, if desired.

Step 7. Cut a slit through one layer only on each arm piece where indicated on pattern; turn arms right side out through the opening and press. Whipstitch the openings closed.

Step 8. Repeat Steps 1–6, leaving the square end open, to make two holly-leaf wings.

Step 9. Machine-stitch a vein line down the center of each leaf.

Step 10. To make the head, glue fleece to the top of the wooden disc or button; trim to fit.

Step 11. Cut a 3¼" circle from pale pink solid fabric; hand-sew a line of stitches ⅛" from edge all around. Do not cut thread.

Step 12. Place the disc, fleece side down, on the inside of the fabric circle; pull thread to gather fabric edges firmly to the center back of the disk and secure thread.

Step 13. Sew black buttons to face for eyes. Use cotton-tip swab to apply blush to cheeks.

Step 14. Sew red beads to the top and side of head using red beading or quilting thread, taking two stitches for each bead.

Step 15. Glue the head to the top edge of the body front; apply a dot of fabric glue to the top of the arm and to the "hand" area; press arm to body front referring to the Placement Diagram for positioning. Repeat for the second arm.

Step 16. Glue end of holly-leaf wings to back of head.

Step 17. Glue white button to back of head to finish or cover raw edges.

Step 18. Cut an 8" piece of red satin ribbon; tie in a bow.

Step 19. Trim ends in a V-cut and glue to body front under face.

Step 20. Starting ¼" from one end of the remainder of the ribbon and using 2 strands of matching thread, sew along the length of the ribbon in a zig-zag pattern with ½" between stitches at each edge as shown in Figure 1, gathering as you sew and stopping ¼" from end.

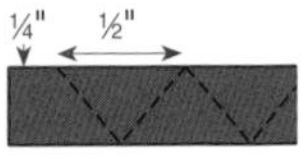

¼"   ½"

Figure 1

Step 21. Pull thread until ribbon fits around the angel skirt, about 1" up from bottom edge. Glue the ruched ribbon to the skirt, overlapping ends at center back.

Step 22. Thread silver ribbon through the hole at the top of the bell; tie ends in a double knot. Glue or tack knot to body between hands.

Step 23. Thread cord through the large-eye embroidery needle; take a small stitch at the top back of the head. Remove cord from needle;

tie ends in knot and trim close to knot to make hanger to finish.

Patchwork Ornament

PROJECT SPECIFICATIONS

Skill Level: Beginner
Ornament Size: 5⅝" x 5⅝" without tassel

MATERIALS

- Scrap red, yellow, blue and green dotted tonals and black-and-white print
- Scrap fleece or needled polyester batting
- All-purpose thread to match fabrics
- Black hand-quilting thread
- No. 5 black pearl cotton
- ¾" red wooden bead with ¼" hole
- 25–36 multicolor glass E beads
- 3½" x 3½" square sturdy cardboard
- Large-eye embroidery needle
- Basic sewing tools and supplies

COMPLETING THE ORNAMENT

Step 1. Cut one 2¼" x 2¼" square from each of the four dotted tonals.

Step 2. Join squares together to make two sets of two squares each; press seams in opposite directions. Join the sets to make a Four-Patch unit.

Step 3. Cut a 4" x 4" square of fleece or batting and black-and-white print for backing.

Step 4. Layer the pieced top, batting and backing with right sides out; pin or baste to hold layers together. Hand-quilt diagonally from corner to corner using black hand-quilting thread.

Step 5. Cut a 2¼" x 22" binding strip black-and-white print. Fold the strip in half with wrong sides together along length and press.

Step 6. Bind edges referring to the General Instructions.

Step 7. To make tassel, wrap the black pearl cotton around the cardboard square about 40 times. Carefully slip the loops off the cardboard and wrap a short piece of

¾"

Figure 2

pearl cotton around the whole bundle about ¾" from top fold; tie off as shown in Figure 2.

Step 8. Cut another short piece; slip it through the top fold. Thread these ends up through the hole in the large red bead and pull to bring tassel top through bead with about ½" above the top as shown in Figure 3. Cut through the fold at the bottom of the tassel so ends hang free.

Figure 3

Step 9. Thread one, two or three E beads on one hanging cord; tie a double knot below beads to hold; repeat until about 12 cords have beads.

Step 10. Thread one end of top cord in needle and take a small stitch at one bottom corner of the patchwork ornament. Tie ends together so tassel hangs just under the corner of the ornament. For hanger, thread an 8" piece of black pearl cotton in needle and take a small stitch in the back top corner opposite the tassel. Tie ends together in a knot; trim close to knot to finish.

Santa Ornament
PROJECT SPECIFICATIONS
Skill Level: Beginner
Ornament Size: 4" x 5¼"

MATERIALS
- Scraps 2 coordinating red-and-white prints, white tonal and pale pink solid
- Scrap fleece
- All-purpose thread to match fabrics
- White hand-quilting thread
- 2 (¼") black buttons
- 1 (6mm) red bead
- 3 small red E beads
- 9" length ⅜"-wide black velvet ribbon
- ⅝" red star button with shank removed
- 5" piece mini holly garland
- 8" length red cord
- Cosmetic blush and cotton-tip swab
- Fabric glue

- Polyester fiberfill
- Large-eye embroidery needle
- Basic sewing tools and supplies

COMPLETING THE ORNAMENT
Note: *If making a quantity of ornaments, sew long strips of fabric together and subcut into 10"-long segments.*

Step 1. Cut one 2" x 10" A strip pale pink solid, one 2½" x 10" B strip of one red-and-white print and one 3" x 10" C strip of the second red-and-white print.

Step 2. Join strips with right sides together in alphabetical order; press seams in one direction.

Step 3. Prepare a template for Santa using pattern given; place the pattern on the wrong side of the A-B-C strip set, matching lines on pattern with seams on the strip, and trace.

Step 4. Fold the strip with right sides together, carefully matching seam lines; pin to hold.

Step 5. Sew all around on the marked line, leaving an opening at one side as marked on pattern.

Step 6. Cut out ¼" from seam; clip curves, turn right side out and stuff firmly with fiberfill. Fold in seam allowance at opening; slipstitch closed.

Step 7. Draw beard and mustache patterns on the wrong side of the white tonal. Fold fabric in half with right sides together and drawn pattern on top; pin to fleece scrap.

Step 8. Stitch all around on marked lines; cut out ⅛" from seam; clip curves and indents. Trim fleece very close to seam on mustache.

Step 9. Cut a slash through one

Angel With Bell Ornament
Placement Diagram
6½" high

Patchwork Ornament
Placement Diagram
5⅝" x 5⅝"
(without tassel)

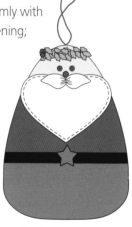
Santa Ornament
Placement Diagram
4" x 5¼"

layer only on each piece as indicated on patterns. Turn right side out through the openings; press. Whipstitch opening closed.

Step 10. Hand-quilt around beard about ¼" from edge with white quilting thread. Hand-sew gathering stitches down the center of the mustache with matching thread; pull tight to gather and wrap thread around the center two times before knotting.

Step 11. Sew black buttons to face for eyes and 6mm red bead for nose. Apply glue to back of beard at top and center, leaving sides free; press in place on face. Glue mustache to the top of the beard directly below the nose.

Step 12. Glue ⅜"-wide black velvet ribbon over body seam, butting ends together at center front. Glue the red star button over the ends.

Step 13. Wrap the holly garland around the top of the head to shape; remove and twist ends together. Place on head with twisted ends in back; tack in place.

Step 14. Sew three small red E beads to garland at one side.

Step 15. For hanger, thread large-eye embroidery needle with red cord; take a small stitch at the top back of the head. Remove cord from needle; tie ends in knot. Clip ends close to knot to finish. ❖

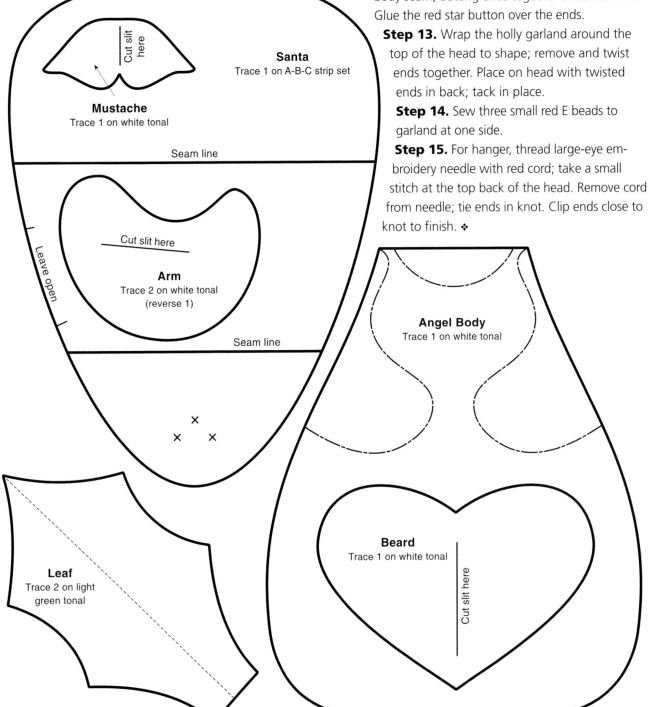

Mustache
Trace 1 on white tonal

Cut slit here

Santa
Trace 1 on A-B-C strip set

Seam line

Cut slit here

Arm
Trace 2 on white tonal
(reverse 1)

Leave open

Seam line

Angel Body
Trace 1 on white tonal

Leaf
Trace 2 on light green tonal

Beard
Trace 1 on white tonal

Cut slit here

Snowman Yo-Yo Lampshade Cover

Design by **CHRIS MALONE**

Dress up a lamp with a holiday cover.

PROJECT SPECIFICATIONS

Skill Level: Intermediate

Cover fits a lampshade with 6" top diameter x 9" high x 13" bottom diameter

MATERIALS

- Scraps orange, red, green, blue and purple felt
- ⅜ yard white tonal
- ⅝ yard black/white dot
- ⅝ yard backing fabric
- 20" x 40" rectangle thin, needled batting
- All-purpose thread to match fabrics
- Orange and white embroidery floss
- Lampshade—9" high, 6" across at top and 13" at bottom
- 1¼ yards white mini-ball-fringe trim
- 1⅓ yards black ¼"-wide grosgrain ribbon
- 10 (6mm) black beads
- 10 (¾") black shank buttons
- 14 (⅝") white buttons
- Newsprint or large sheet of paper for pattern
- 80" silver color 18-gauge wire
- Fabric glue
- Wire cutters
- Needle-nose pliers
- Compass
- Basic sewing tools and supplies

MAKING THE COVER

Step 1. Place seam of lampshade ½" from edge of newsprint or paper. Carefully roll the shade across the paper, marking paper along the top and bottom edges of the shade as it moves; stop when you return to the seam.

Step 2. Add ½" seam allowance to the straight end and ⅜" to the top and bottom curved edges.

Step 3. Cut one shade cover each from black/white dot, backing fabric and batting using the paper pattern.

Step 4. Cut the black ribbon into six 8" lengths. Pin ends of three lengths down each straight edge of the shade cover, positioning one piece ⅜" from the top, one ⅜" from the bottom and one in the center as shown in Figure 1; machine-baste to hold in place.

⅜"

⅜"

Figure 1

Step 5. Place the shade cover and backing pieces right sides together with ribbon pieces between the layers; pin these layers to the batting. Stitch all around, leaving an opening between two ribbons on one back edge.

Step 6. Trim batting close to seam; trim corners and clip curves. Turn right side out; press at edges to flatten.

Step 7. Fold in seam allowance at the opening edges; press and slipstitch to close.

MAKING THE YO-YO SNOWMEN

Step 1. Using the compass, draw five circles each 4", 5½" and 6½" onto the wrong side of the white tonal; cut out.

Step 2. Repeat to cut five circles each 1¾", 2¼" and 3" from batting.

Step 3. Center and pin from the right side the small, medium and large batting circles on the wrong side of corresponding white fabric circles; for example, center the 1¾" batting circle on the 4" fabric circle.

Step 4. To complete one yo-yo, fold the raw edge to the back side ¼"; finger-press to hold.

Step 5. Using a needle threaded with a double, knotted thread, sew a running stitch along the edge of the folded-under edge as shown in Figure 2.

Figure 2   Figure 3

Step 6. Pull the thread to gather tightly, positioning the hole in the center as shown in Figure 3. Repeat for each circle.

Step 7. Sew a black shank button to the center of each medium and large yo-yo. Sew two black beads to each small yo-yo for eyes referring to the close-up photo of snowman motif for positioning.

Step 8. To make one snowman motif, arrange one small, medium and large yo-yo, overlapping edges as shown in Figure 4; glue to hold using fabric glue.

Figure 4

Step 9. Prepare templates for scarf and nose using patterns given; cut as directed on each piece.

Step 10. Layer two nose pieces together; blanket-stitch around edges with 2 strands of orange embroidery floss to join layers together. Repeat to make five noses.

Step 11. Using fabric glue, glue a nose to each small yo-yo to cover the center hole.

Step 12. Wrap one scarf piece around the neck of one snowman between the small and medium yo-yos and glue ends to the back side with fabric glue.

Step 13. Cut one ⅝" x 5" strip from each color felt for scarf ends. Tie a knot in the center of each strip, clip ends in ½" to make fringe and glue the knot to the side of a matching scarf to complete the snowman motifs.

COMPLETING THE COVER

Step 1. Lay the lampshade cover out flat on a work surface. Arrange snowman motifs evenly around the cover with bottom yo-yo about 1" above bottom of cover and bodies about 4" apart. When satisfied with the arrangement, glue in place with fabric glue. **Note:** *It is not necessary to apply glue out to the edges; use just enough glue to secure.*

Step 2. Cut wire into (10) 8" lengths using wire cutters.

Step 3. Use needle-nose pliers to curl the tip of each length of wire. Then use your fingers to turn the wire, shaping irregular concentric circles using pattern given as a guide, leaving 2" of the wire straight. Repeat to make 10 wire arms.

Step 4. Apply a thin line of fabric glue in a gathered fold on each side of each medium yo-yo and slip the straight end of the wire into the fold. Add wire arms to each side of each snowman.

Step 5. Randomly sew white buttons to the background to simulate snowflakes using white embroidery floss.

Step 6. Sew or glue the ball fringe to the bottom edge of the shade cover.

Step 7. Wrap the shade cover around the lampshade, tying with ribbons on the back side to use. ❖

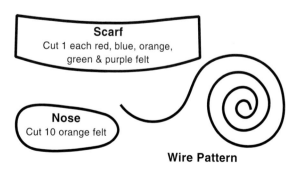

Scarf
Cut 1 each red, blue, orange,
green & purple felt

Nose
Cut 10 orange felt

Wire Pattern

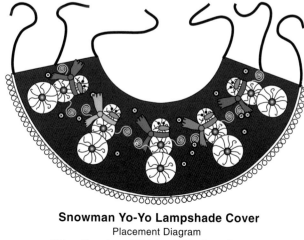

Snowman Yo-Yo Lampshade Cover
Placement Diagram
6" top diameter x 9" high x 13" bottom diameter

Poinsettia Holiday Card Holder

Design by **WILLOW ANN SIRCH**

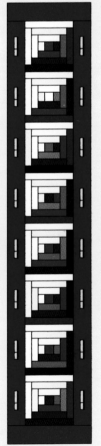

**Poinsettia Holiday
Card Holder**
Placement Diagram
9½" x 48"

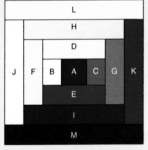

Courthouse Steps
5½" x 5½" Block

Display your holiday cards on this simple card holder.

- Batting 16" x 54"
- All-purpose thread to match fabrics
- Gold metallic thread
- 16 mini-clothespins
- Gold spray paint
- Basic sewing tools and supplies

PROJECT SPECIFICATIONS

Skill Level: Beginner
Holder Size: 9½" x 48"
Block Size: 5½" x 5½"
Number of Blocks: 8

MATERIALS

- 8–10 fat quarters or scraps holiday reds, greens and whites/creams
- ¼ yard red tonal
- ⅓ yard red/gold print
- Backing 15" x 54" and 3" x 9½" strip for sleeve

CUTTING

Step 1. Cut eight 1½" x 1½" A squares red scraps.

Step 2. Cut 1¼"-wide strips from the fat quarters or scraps. To start, cut two or three strips from each fat quarter or scrap and cut more as needed.

Step 3. Subcut the 1¼"-wide white/cream strips into eight of each of the following pieces: 1½" B, 3" D and F, 4½" H and J and 6" L.

Step 4. Subcut the 1¼"-wide red strips into eight of each of the following pieces: 1½" C, 3" E and G and 4½" I.

Step 5. Subcut the 1¼"-wide green strips into eight of each of the following pieces: 4½" K and 6" M.

Step 6. Cut three 2½" by fabric width strips red/gold print. Join strips on short ends to make one long strip; press seams open. Subcut strip into two 44½" N strips and two 10" O strips.

Step 7. Cut three 2¼" by fabric width strips red tonal for binding.

COMPLETING THE BLOCKS

Step 1. To complete one Courthouse Steps block, sew B and C to opposite sides of A; press seams away from A.

Step 2. Continue to add pieces to opposite sides of the center unit in alphabetical order, keeping light pieces on one side and dark pieces on the opposite side, to complete one Courthouse Steps block; press seams toward the newly added strip before adding consecutive strips. Repeat to make eight blocks.

COMPLETING THE HOLDER

Step 1. Join the Courthouse Steps blocks referring to the Placement Diagram for positioning; press seams in one direction.

Step 2. Sew an N strip to opposite long sides and O strips to the top and bottom of the pieced center to complete the pieced top; press seams toward the N and O strips.

Step 3. Complete the holder using gold metallic thread for quilting referring to Completing Your Quilt on page 173.

Step 4. Spray-paint the front and sides of the mini-clothespins with gold spray paint; let dry.

Step 5. Position and hand-stitch the painted clothespins in place through the metal hinge along the side border strips referring to the Placement Diagram and project photo for positioning.

Step 6. Fold each raw edge of the sleeve strip under ¼"; stitch to hold.

Step 7. Hand-stitch the sleeve to the top back-side edge of the completed holder to hang. ❖

Gift-Wrapped Toilet Seat Cover

Design by **CONNIE KAUFFMAN**

Dress up your bathroom with a Christmas cover.

PROJECT SPECIFICATIONS
Skill Level: Intermediate
Cover Size: Size varies
Block Size: 3¾" x 4¾"
Number of Blocks: 4

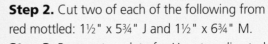

Gift Wrap
3¾" x 4¾" Block

MATERIALS
- ⅛ yard red print
- ⅛ yard red mottled
- ½ yard green print
- Backing 22" x 24"
- Batting 22" x 24"
- All-purpose thread to match fabrics
- Red and green quilting thread
- 30" (¼"-wide) elastic
- Lightweight cardboard for cover pattern
- Basic sewing tools and supplies

CUTTING
Step 1. Cut two of each of the following from green print: 10½" x 5¾" I; 4¼" x 5¾" K; 9½" x 6¾" L; and 4¼" x 6¾" N.

Step 2. Cut two of each of the following from red mottled: 1½" x 5¾" J and 1½" x 6¾" M.

Step 3. Prepare template for H; cut as directed.

COMPLETING THE BLOCKS
Step 1. Prepare five copies of each of the paper-piecing patterns given. Cut one copy of each pattern apart to make seven individual pattern pieces. Use these pieces to cut four fabric pieces for each shape in the colors marked on the pattern, adding ½" all around when cutting as shown in Figure 1.

Figure 1

Step 2. Shorten the stitch length on your machine to 18–20 stitches per inch.

Step 3. Beginning with the A-B section, place fabric to cover area A on the paper pattern with wrong side of fabric against the unmarked side of the paper.

Step 4. Place fabric for area B right sides together with piece A on the A-B edge as shown in Figure 2; pin along the A-B line. Fold piece B over to cover area B as shown in Figure 3; adjust fabric if necessary. Unfold piece B to lie flat on piece A.

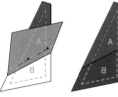

Figure 2   **Figure 3**

Step 5. Flip paper pattern; stitch on the A-B line, stitching to (or beyond) the outside outer edges as shown in Figure 4.

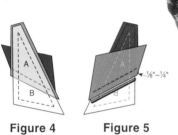

Figure 4   **Figure 5**

Step 6. Trim the A-B seam allowance to ⅛"–¼" as shown in Figure 5. Fold piece B to cover area B; lightly press with a warm dry iron.

Step 7. Repeat with remaining sections.

Step 8. Pin outside fabric edges to the paper pattern. Trim fabric edges along solid line of paper pattern as shown in Figure 6.

Figure 6   **Figure 7**

Step 9. Join one of each paper-pieced section with H to complete one block as shown in Figure 7.

Step 10. Repeat Steps 1–9 to complete four Gift Wrap blocks.

COMPLETING THE COVER

Step 1. Sew J between I and K to complete an I-J-K section as shown in Figure 8; press seams away from J. Repeat to make two I-J-K sections.

Figure 8

Step 2. Sew M between L and N to complete an L-M-N section, again referring to Figure 8; press seams away from M. Repeat to make two L-M-N sections.

GIFT-WRAPPED TOILET SEAT COVER

Step 3. Starting with a partial seam, join the four Gift Wrap blocks as shown in Figure 9 to complete the pieced center, adding blocks in a clockwise direction and completing the partial seam; press seams in one direction. ***Note:*** *There will be an opening in the center.*

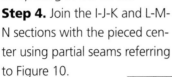

Figure 9

Step 4. Join the I-J-K and L-M-N sections with the pieced center using partial seams referring to Figure 10.

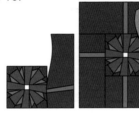

Figure 10

Step 5. Place the two circle pieces right sides together; sew all around using a ¼" seam allowance; trim close to seam.

Step 6. Cut an opening in one of the fabric circles and turn right side out through the opening; press flat.

Step 7. Center and hand-stitch the circle on the pieced center.

Step 8. Trace your toilet seat lid onto lightweight cardboard; add 2½" all around as shown in Figure 11.

Figure 11

Step 9. Cut a batting and backing piece using the cardboard pattern.

Step 10. Lay the batting on a flat surface; place the backing piece right side up on the batting. Measure and mark 2" from edge of backing all around; stitch on the marked line.

Gift-Wrapped Toilet Seat Cover
Placement Diagram
Size Varies

Step 11. Trim the batting close to the stitched line.

Step 12. Lay the stitched batting/backing section right sides together with the front pieced section as shown in Figure 12; stitch around curved edges, leaving the straight back edge open.

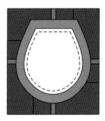

Figure 12

Step 13. Trim the front pieced section even with the backing/batting section. Turn right side out through back-edge opening.

Step 14. Turn the fabric along the straight edge ½" to the inside; pin to hold.

Step 15. Sew close to the outside curved edge and ½" from the outside edge to make the elastic casing as shown in Figure 13.

Figure 13

Step 16. Stitch a ½" seam along the straight back edge between the stitched casing lines, again referring to Figure 13.

Step 17. Machine-quilt in the ditch around the red bow pieces with red quilting thread.

Step 18. Thread the elastic through the casing, leaving 4"–5" extending from each end.

Step 19. Slip the cover on the toilet lid and draw up the elastic to fit; tie ends. Machine-stitch the ends of the elastic to the cover to keep it from slipping back inside the casing when washed.

Step 20. If desired, gather the straight edge of the cover to draw the cover in for a tighter fit to finish. ❖

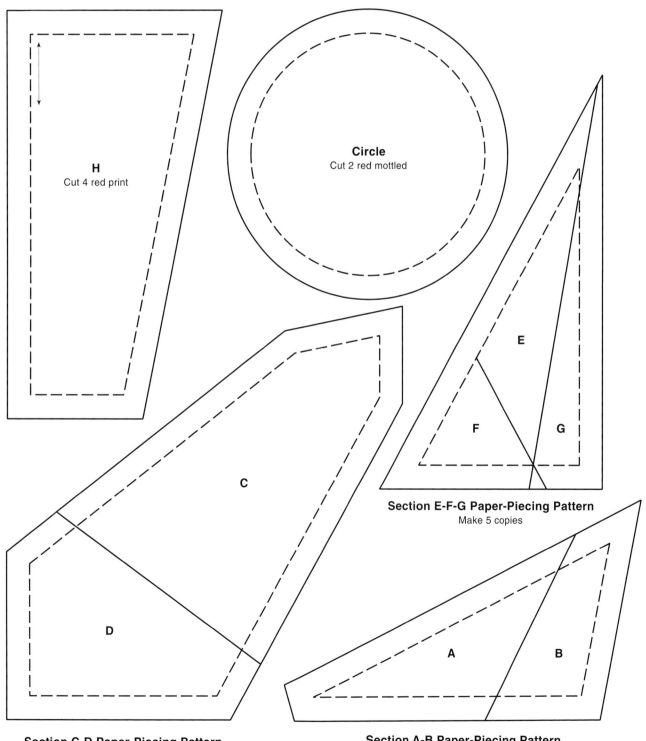

H
Cut 4 red print

Circle
Cut 2 red mottled

E

F

G

Section E-F-G Paper-Piecing Pattern
Make 5 copies

C

D

A

B

Section C-D Paper-Piecing Pattern
Make 5 copies

Section A-B Paper-Piecing Pattern
Make 5 copies

Holiday Fun Candle Mat

Design by **ROCHELLE MARTIN, COTTAGE QUILT DESIGNS**

Felt or felted wool makes the perfect fabric for appliquéd snowflakes and snowmen in this cute little wintertime candle mat.

PROJECT SPECIFICATIONS

Skill Level: Beginner
Mat Size: 12" x 12"
Block Size: 6" x 6"
Number of blocks: 4

MATERIALS

- ⅛ yard green felt or felted wool
- ¼ yard red plaid
- ¼ yard green print
- ¼ yard red mottled
- ¼ yard white felt or felted wool
- Thin batting 15" x 15"
- Neutral color all-purpose thread
- Gold metallic thread
- Black No. 8 pearl cotton
- ⅓ yard fusible web
- Small, sharp scissors
- Basic sewing tools and supplies

CUTTING

Step 1. Cut one 6½" by fabric width strip each green print (A) and red mottled (B); subcut each strip into four 6½" squares.

Step 2. Cut two 2¼" by fabric width strips red plaid for binding.

Step 3. Trace the individual appliqué shapes onto the paper side of the fusible web referring to patterns for number to cut, leaving ½" between shapes. Cut out shapes, leaving a margin around each one.

Step 4. Fuse shapes to felt or felted wool as directed on patterns for color; cut out shapes on traced lines. Remove paper backing.

COMPLETING THE MAT

Step 1. Fold and crease each A and B square to mark the centers.

Step 2. Sew an A square to a B square; press

seam toward B. Repeat to make two A-B rows. Join the rows to complete the A-B background as shown in Figure 1; repeat to make a second A-B backing. Press seams in one direction.

Figure 1

Step 3. Center and fuse a snowflake in each A square.

Step 4. Using 1 strand of black pearl cotton, blanket-stitch around the fused snowflake designs and inside the cut-out circles in the center as shown in Figure 2.

Figure 2

Step 5. Transfer the snowman face features to the snowman body pieces. Using 1 strand of black pearl cotton, backstitch mouths and eyebrows and add French knots for eyes and noses.

Blanket Stitch

Backstitch

French Knot

Holiday Fun Candle Mat
Placement Diagram
12" x 12"

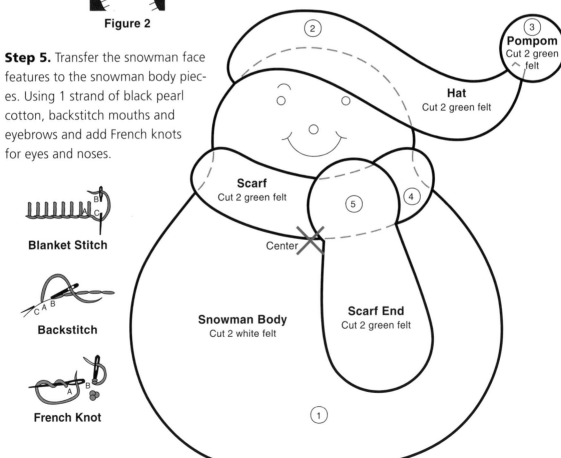

②

③ **Pompom**
Cut 2 green
felt

Hat
Cut 2 green felt

Scarf
Cut 2 green felt

④ ⑤

Center ✕

Snowman Body
Cut 2 white felt

Scarf End
Cut 2 green felt

①

Step 6. Center and fuse a snowman motif to each B square with snowman 2¼" from the diagonal corner of B as shown in Figure 3. Position hat so that the pompom lies on the seam line between the A and B squares as shown in Figure 4.

Figure 3

Figure 4

Step 7. Blanket-stitch around each shape as in Step 4 to complete the top.

Step 8. Complete the mat using the A-B backing piece referring to Completing Your Quilt on page 173 and using gold metallic thread to hand-quilt ⅛" away from the appliqué shapes. ❖

Snowflake 2
Cut 1 white felt

Snowflake 1
Cut 1 white felt

Sliding Penguins Apron

Design by **CONNIE KAUFFMAN**

Make this apron to wear during holiday preparations.

PROJECT SPECIFICATIONS

Skill Level: Beginner
Apron Size: One size fits all

MATERIALS

- 4" x 4" scraps white sparkle and yellow, blue, peach, green and pink pastels
- 2" x 2" scrap orange solid
- 3" x 3" scrap gray sparkle
- 4" x 4" scrap each white and black mottleds
- ¼ yard silver crepe
- 1⅝ yards blue mottled
- Thin batting 26" x 29"
- Silver, black, white, orange and blue all-purpose thread
- Silver metallic thread
- Invisible thread
- 2 (¾") blue buttons
- 4 black seed beads
- 24" x 27" piece paper to make apron pattern
- Appliqué pressing sheet
- ½ yard fusible web
- Basic sewing tools and supplies

CUTTING

Step 1. Cut one 2½" x 30" neck-strap strip and two 4½" x 29½" tie strips along the length of the blue mottled.

Step 2. Fold the pattern paper in half along the 27" length. Referring to Figure 1, measure 18" up and 2½" in on the unfolded edge and mark. Draw a straight line from the mark to the bottom corner. Measure 5½" over from the folded top corner and mark; draw a straight line 6" down from this mark. Connect this line to the line on the side edge with a straight diagonal line. Trim excess paper beyond the marked lines.

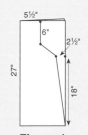

Figure 1

Step 3. Mark a gently curving line from the side edge to the bib edge as shown in Figure 2; trim on the line. Round the skirt bottom corner and bib top corner and unfold paper to complete the apron pattern.

Figure 2

Step 4. Cut one apron shape from thin batting and two from blue mottled.

Step 5. Trace appliqué shapes given, except igloo, onto the paper side of the fusible web referring to pattern for number to cut. Prepare a pattern for the igloo shape.

Step 6. Cut out shapes, leaving a margin around each one.

Step 7. Fuse paper shapes to the wrong side of fabrics as directed on pieces for color and number to cut. Cut out shapes on traced lines; remove paper backing.

Step 8. Bond fusible web to the wrong side of the white sparkle, peach, green, pink, yellow

and blue scraps and a 4" x 4" square of silver crepe; cut scraps and silver crepe into ¾"–1" squares and rectangles for igloo appliqué.

COMPLETING THE APPLIQUÉ
Step 1. Using the appliqué pressing sheet, assemble a penguin motif and a reversed penguin motif in numerical order referring to the full-size motif; set aside.

Step 2. Place the igloo pattern under the appliqué pressing sheet.

Step 3. Arrange and fuse the igloo scraps on

SLIDING PENGUINS APRON

the appliqué pressing sheet to resemble bricks using the pattern beneath as a guide and overlapping pieces referring to the close-up photo. **Note:** *Let the squares go beyond the edges of the pattern to trim later; do not cover door opening with scraps.*

Figure 3

Step 4. Lay the igloo pattern on the fused piece and trim as shown in Figure 3.

Step 5. Arrange and fuse door piece in place.

Step 6. Arrange and fuse the appliqué pieces and motifs on the apron front referring to the Placement Diagram for positioning, placing the igloo 3¾" down from the top edge.

Step 7. Using silver metallic thread, machine buttonhole-stitch around each swirl shape. Repeat with thread to match fabrics on penguins and igloo shapes.

Step 8. Machine-stitch the hair lines on penquin heads with black thread and a narrow zigzag stitch.

Step 9. Sew a black seed bead to the center of each eye on each penguin.

COMPLETING THE APRON

Step 1. Fold the neck-strap piece with right sides together along the length; stitch along long raw edge, leaving a 2" opening and rounding ends as you stitch as shown in Figure 4.

Figure 4

Step 2. Clip curves; turn right side out and press. Turn opening seam in ¼"; hand-stitch opening closed.

Step 3. Fold each tie strap with right sides

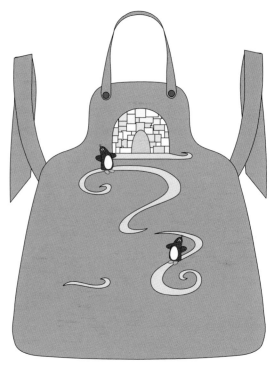

Sliding Penguins Apron
Placement Diagram
One Size Fits All

together along the length; stitch along the long edge and across one end, angling seam as you stitch as shown in Figure 5.

Figure 5

Step 4. Trim end seam, clip corners and turn right side out; press.

Step 5. Pin and baste the raw end of a tie on each side edge on the right side of the apron front as shown in Figure 6.

Figure 6

Step 6. Lay the batting down on a flat surface with backing piece right side up on top; lay the appliquéd apron front right sides together with batting/backing layers with strap ends between the layers.

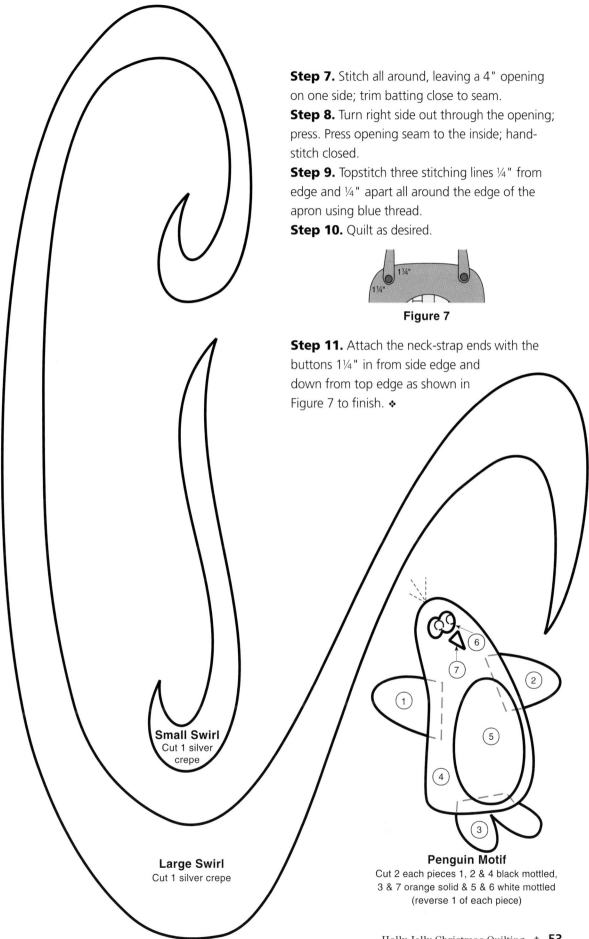

Step 7. Stitch all around, leaving a 4" opening on one side; trim batting close to seam.

Step 8. Turn right side out through the opening; press. Press opening seam to the inside; hand-stitch closed.

Step 9. Topstitch three stitching lines ¼" from edge and ¼" apart all around the edge of the apron using blue thread.

Step 10. Quilt as desired.

1¼"

1¼"

Figure 7

Step 11. Attach the neck-strap ends with the buttons 1¼" in from side edge and down from top edge as shown in Figure 7 to finish. ❖

Small Swirl
Cut 1 silver crepe

Large Swirl
Cut 1 silver crepe

Penguin Motif
Cut 2 each pieces 1, 2 & 4 black mottled,
3 & 7 orange solid & 5 & 6 white mottled
(reverse 1 of each piece)

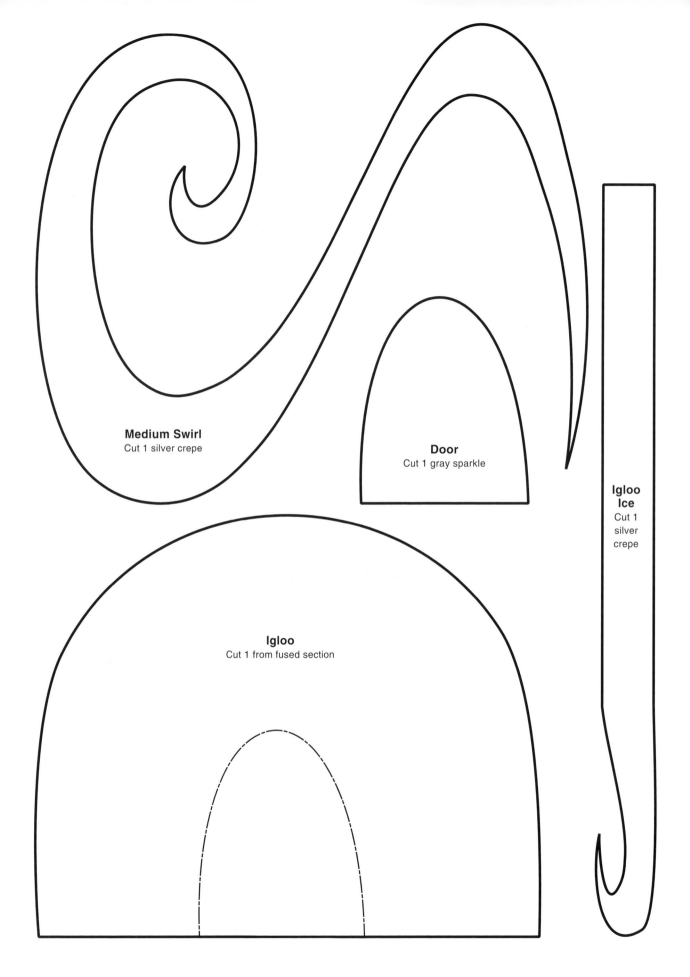

Medium Swirl
Cut 1 silver crepe

Door
Cut 1 gray sparkle

Igloo Ice
Cut 1 silver crepe

Igloo
Cut 1 from fused section

Mad About Scraps Christmas Apron

Design by **WILLOW ANN SIRCH**

Use up a variety of festive holiday scraps to make a simple apron.

PROJECT SPECIFICATIONS
Skill Level: Beginner
Apron Size: 31½" x 33"

MATERIALS
- Assorted scraps in a mix of small, medium and large holiday prints
- 10" x 10" A square muslin
- 24" x 32" B rectangle muslin
- 1¼ yards backing fabric
- Neutral color all-purpose thread
- Gold metallic thread
- 2" strip hook-and-loop tape
- Basic sewing tools and supplies

CUTTING
Step 1. Cut 25–30 rectangles approximately 6"–8" x 7"–10" from the assorted holiday prints.

COMPLETING THE APRON FRONT
Step 1. Center and stitch A to one 32" edge of B to complete the foundation; press seam toward A.
Step 2. Fold the foundation in half and press to mark the center.
Step 3. Working from the center out, position one fabric rectangle on the foundation as shown in Figure 1.

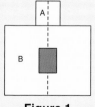

Figure 1   **Figure 2**

Step 4. Fold under one edge of a second fabric rectangle ¼"; press. Position it next to the first rectangle with the folded edge of rectangle 2 covering one raw edge of rectangle 1 as shown in Figure 2.

Step 5. Pin, iron and topstitch the folded edge of rectangle 2 in place.

Step 6. Continue to position rectangles, fold, press and stitch edges under so one or two folded edges cover the raw edge of one or more rectangles already in place, working your way from the center to the outer edges and leaving outside edges unturned until the foundation has been covered.

Step 7. Trim all patchwork even with the edge of the foundation.

COMPLETING THE APRON

Step 1. Place the backing fabric right side up on a flat surface; pin the stitched apron right sides together with the backing piece. Trim backing even with apron front.

Step 2. Stitch all around, leaving a 4" opening on the bottom edge. Clip corners and into indent between the apron top and bottom as shown in Figure 3.

Mad About Scraps Christmas Apron
Placement Diagram
31½" x 33"

Figure 3

Step 3. Turn right side out through the opening; press.

Step 4. Turn in seam at opening; hand-stitch opening closed.

Step 5. Topstitch ¼" from edge all around.

Step 6. Cut one 2½" x 24" neck strap from leftover backing fabric.

Step 7. Cut two 1½" x 24" tie strips from leftover backing fabric.

Step 8. Fold the neck and tie straps in half with right sides together along the length; stitch along length. Turn right side out; press with seams on the side.

Step 9. Fold the end of each tie strap over ¼" and then ¼" again; stitch to finish ends.

Step 10. Secure one end of each tie strap on the wrong side of the apron at the top of each side.

Step 11. Fold the raw ends of the neck strap in ¼" and stitch across ends to finish.

Step 12. Stitch one end of the neck strap to one top back-side corner of the apron bib ½" from side edge as shown in Figure 4.

Figure 4

Step 13. Stitch the loop end of the hook-and-loop tape to the remaining top back-side corner of the apron bib ½" from side edge.

Figure 5

Step 14. Stitch the hook part of the hook-and-loop tape to the center of the wrong side of the neck strap as shown in Figure 5 to finish. ❖

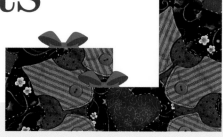

Holly Wreath Chair Jackets

Design by **JODI G. WARNER**

Decorate the tops of your chairs with holiday flair.

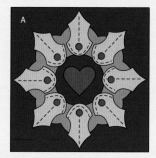

Holly Wreath
9¾" x 9¾" Block

PROJECT NOTES

Chair jackets are designed for standard ladder-back–style chairs measuring approximately 14" between the side rails. The decorative panel is placed on the back for best visibility. In these instructions "back" refers to the appliqué panel and "front" refers to the plain panel, which may be concealed by a sitting person.

The materials and instructions result in two matching chair jackets.

PROJECT SPECIFICATIONS

Skill Level: Intermediate
Jacket Size: 16¼" x 17¼"
Block Size: 9¾" x 9¾"
Number of Blocks: 2

MATERIALS

Makes 2 chair jackets.
- Scrap red tonal
- ⅛ yard green/black homespun stripe
- ⅓ yard green dot tonal
- ½ yard red homespun stripe
- ½ yard green stripe tonal
- ⅝ yard black holly print
- 2⅓ yards red dot tonal
- Batting 4 (18" x 19") rectangles
- All-purpose thread to match fabrics
- Green and white quilting thread
- 16 (½") red buttons
- Temporary marking tool
- Basic sewing tools and supplies

CUTTING

Step 1. Cut two 10¼" x 10¼" A squares black holly print; fold in quarters and along both diagonals and crease to mark center guidelines. Transfer wreath position from pattern to the right side of each square.

Step 2. Prepare templates for appliqué pieces using patterns given; cut wreaths and hearts as directed on each piece, adding ¼" all around each piece when cutting. Do not cut leaves at this time.

Step 3. Cut one 5¾" by fabric width strip green stripe tonal; subcut strip into (16) 2" M tie strips.

Step 4. Cut two 4" by fabric width strips green stripe tonal for leaves.

Step 5. Cut six 1¼" x 8½" strips black holly print (B) and seven strips red homespun stripe (C).

Step 6. Cut eight 1¼" x 10¼" D strips red homespun stripe.

Step 7. Cut eight 1¾" x 1¾" E squares green dot tonal.

Step 8. Cut four 1" x 12¾" F strips and four 1" x 13¾" G strips green/black homespun stripe.

Step 9. Cut four 2" x 13¾" H strips, two 2" x 16¾" I strips and two 3" x 16¾" J strips red dot tonal.

Step 10. Cut four 2" x 17¾" K strips and four 2" x 16¾" L strips red dot tonal.

Step 11. Cut two 18" x 19" N rectangles red dot tonal.

Step 12. Cut one 2½" x 16" O strip red dot tonal.

Step 13. Cut two 18" x 38" P strips red dot tonal.

Step 14. Cut three 1⅛" by fabric width strips red dot tonal for binding.

COMPLETING THE BLOCKS

Step 1. Trace the leaf template onto the wrong side of one green stripe tonal strip as directed on pattern for number to cut, leaving ¼" between shapes.

Step 2. Place the marked strip right sides together with the remaining green stripe tonal strip; pin to hold.

Step 3. Reduce machine-stitch length to 12–15 stitches per inch or 1.5mm.

Step 4. Stitch on the marked leaf lines through both layers; cut out each leaf, leaving a ⅛"–¼" seam allowance all around.

Step 5. Clip inside curved edges and trim excess at points.

Step 6. Carefully cut a 1" slit in the back side of each leaf as shown in Figure 1; turn right side out through the opening, working points and curves out. Press.

Figure 1

Step 7. Prepare the wreath pieces for appliqué

referring to the General Instructions (page 173) for hand appliqué.

Step 8. Center and pin a wreath shape on each A square referring to Figure 2; hand-stitch in place.

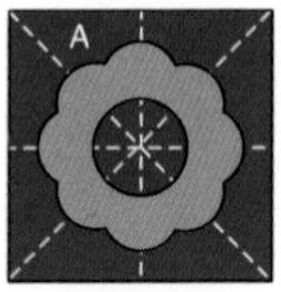

Figure 2

Step 9. Prepare hearts for appliqué; center and stitch one shape in each wreath.

Step 10. Arrange and pin eight leaf shapes over each wreath with rounded ends slightly beyond the inner edge as marked on the pattern and points at the quarter and diagonal creased lines as shown in Figure 3. **Note:** *Leaves should be evenly spaced.*

Figure 3

Step 11. Referring to Figure 4, topstitch leaves in place.

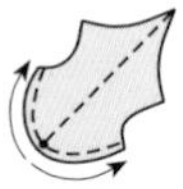

Figure 4

Step 12. Sew a red button on each leaf to complete the blocks referring to the block drawing for positioning.

COMPLETING THE CHAIR JACKETS

Step 1. Join the B and C strips, starting and ending with C, to complete a strip set; press seams toward B strips.

Step 2. Subcut the B-C strip set into eight 1" B-C strips as shown in Figure 5.

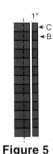

Figure 5

Step 3. Sew a B-C strip set to a D strip as shown in Figure 6; press seams toward the D strip. Repeat to make eight B-C-D strips.

Figure 6

Step 4. Sew a B-C-D strip to opposite sides of one block; press seams toward strips.

Step 5. Sew an E square to each end of two B-C-D strips; press seams away from E squares.

Step 6. Sew a B-C-D-E strip to the remaining sides of the block; press seams toward strips.

Step 7. Sew an F strip to opposite sides and G strips to the remaining sides of the pieced center; press seams toward F and G strips.

Step 8. Sew an H strip to opposite sides, the I strip to the top and the J strip to the bottom of the pieced center; press seams toward the H, I and J strips to complete one chair back. Repeat to make two chair backs.

Step 9. Transfer the quilting design given to the H, I and J strips.

Step 10. Mark diagonal quilting lines 1" apart on A and a 1½" diagonal grid on each N rectangle.

Step 11. Prepare the completed back pieces for quilting and quilt on marked lines and around the wreath and heart shapes by hand or machine; trim edges even with the pieced-and-appliquéd back piece.

Step 12. Fold each M strip with right sides together; stitch along the length and across one end; clip corners. Turn right side out; press with seam on one side to complete tie strips.

Step 13. Position four tie strips over each back

panel with raw edges matched to panel side raw edges, 1¾" down from upper raw edge and 6¼" up from lower raw edge as shown in Figure 7.

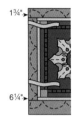

Figure 7

Step 14. Press under ¼" on one long raw edge of each K and L strip.

Step 15. Position and pin one K strip right sides together at each back panel side edge with raw edges aligned and ties between layers; stitch. Press strip to the back side; hand-stitch folded edge in place.

Step 16. Position and pin L strips right sides together at the top and bottom edges of the back panel; stitch. Press strip toward the back side; turn ends in ¼" and hand-stitch folded edge in place.

Step 17. Fold a P strip in half across the width to make an 18" x 19" rectangle; mark a 1½" diagonal grid on the rectangle. Insert a batting piece between the layers.

Step 18. Quilt on the marked lines. Trim the quilted rectangle to 16¼" x 17¼" to complete one front panel; do not trim the folded edge. Repeat to make the second front panel.

Step 19. Position four M tie strips on the side edges of the front panels, with raw edges aligned, 1½" down from top raw edge and 6" up from folded bottom edge.

Step 20. Join the binding strips on short ends with diagonal seams to make a long binding strip; press seams open.

Step 21. Fold under one long raw edge of the binding strip ¼"; press.

Step 22. Stitch the binding strip to the wrong side (without the tie strips) of one front panel, beginning at one folded bottom edge corner, leaving ¼" excess, and ending at the other corner, mitering corners and trimming to leave ¼" excess as shown in Figure 8.

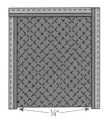

Figure 8

Step 23. Press bias strip to the right side of the front panel, over the raw ends of the tie strips as shown in Figure 9; turn raw ends to the inside ¼" and topstitch binding in place from the right side of the front panel. Pull the tie strips over binding; hand-stitch at binding edge to hold in place.

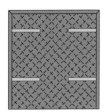

Figure 9

Step 24. Fold the O strip with right sides together along the length; stitch along the raw edge to make a tube; turn right side out. Press with seam centered on the back side. Cut into four 3¾" connector strips.

Step 25. Turn each end of each connector strip to the inside ¼" and press.

Figure 10

Step 26. Position an O connector strip 1" down from the top edge and 1¼" from side edges of one front and one back panel; pin and hand-stitch edges of strips in place to finish as shown in Figure 10. ❖

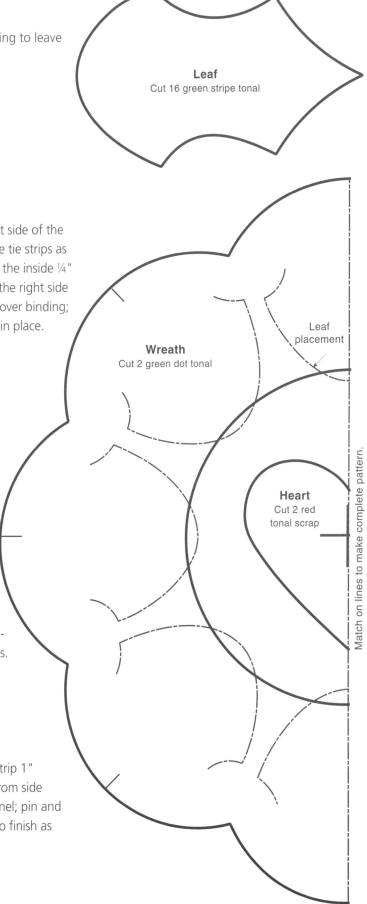

Leaf
Cut 16 green stripe tonal

Leaf placement

Wreath
Cut 2 green dot tonal

Heart
Cut 2 red tonal scrap

Match on lines to make complete pattern.

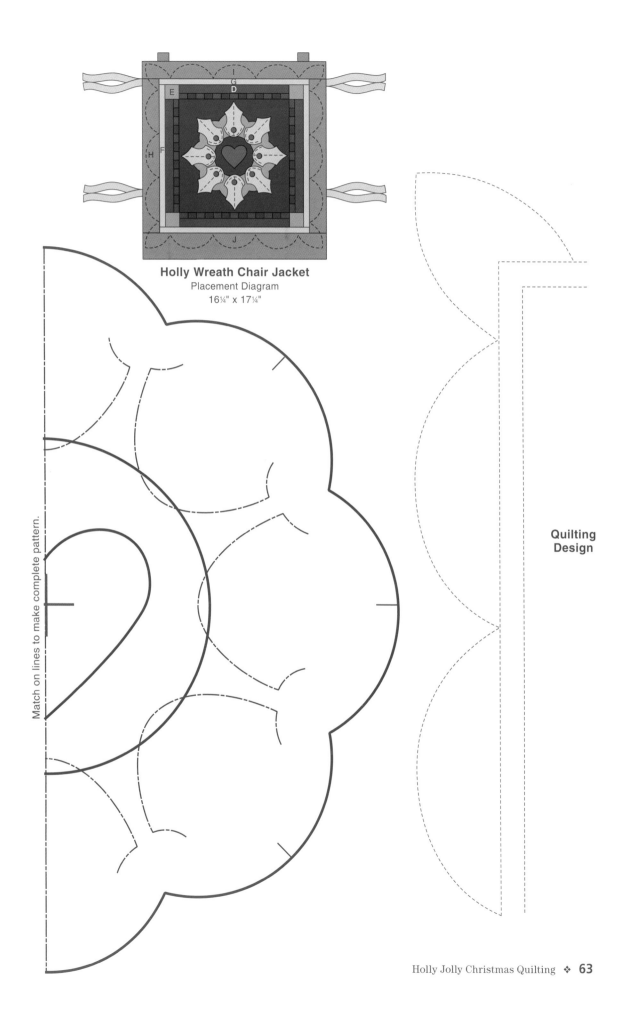

Holly Wreath Chair Jacket
Placement Diagram
16¼" x 17¼"

Quilting
Design

Match on lines to make complete pattern.

Holly Party Set

Designs by **JILL REBER**

Make a table topper and matching hot pad with simple holly shapes.

Holly Leaf
8" x 8" Block

PROJECT SPECIFICATIONS

Skill Level: Beginner
Topper Size: 30" x 30"
Mat Size: 8½" x 8½"
Block Size: 8" x 8"
Number of Blocks: 5

MATERIALS

- Medium and dark green tonal scraps
- 3 different dark red tonal scraps
- ⅓ yard red tonal
- ½ yard tan check tonal
- ½ yard green tonal
- 1 yard cream holly print
- Batting 36" x 36" and 8½" x 8½"
- All-purpose thread to match fabrics
- ⅜ yard fusible web
- Basic sewing tools and supplies

CUTTING

Step 1. Prepare templates for appliqué shapes using patterns given; trace shapes onto the paper side of the fusible web as directed on patterns for number to cut for topper and mat. Cut out shapes, leaving a margin around each one.

Step 2. Fuse shapes to the wrong side of fabrics as directed on patterns for color; cut out shapes on traced lines. Remove paper backing.

Step 3. Cut five 8½" x 8½" A squares tan check tonal.

Step 4. Cut one 8½" by fabric width strip red tonal; subcut strip into (12) 2½" B strips.

Step 5. Cut one 2½" by fabric width strip green tonal; subcut strip into nine 2½" C squares.

Step 6. Cut four 2¼" by fabric width strips green tonal for binding.

Step 7. Cut two 4½" x 22½" D strips and two 4½" x 30½" E strips cream holly print.

Step 8. Cut one 10½" x 10½" backing square cream holly print.

COMPLETING THE TOPPER

Step 1. Arrange leaf and berry shapes on the A squares with points ¾" from the edges of A and overlapping leaf edges as shown in Figure 1; fuse in place to complete the blocks. Set aside one block for hot mat.

Figure 1

Figure 2

Step 2. Join two Holly Leaf blocks with three B strips to make a block row referring to Figure 2; press seams toward B strips. Repeat to make two rows.

Step 3. Join three C squares with two B strips to make a sashing row as shown in Figure 3; press seams toward B strips. Repeat to make three sashing rows.

C B

Figure 3

Step 4. Join the block rows with the sashing rows to complete the pieced center; press seams toward the sashing rows.

Step 5. Sew a D strip to opposite sides and E strips to the top and bottom of the pieced center; press seams toward D and E strips to complete the pieced top.

Step 6. Complete the quilt referring to Completing Your Quilt on page 173.

Step 7. Using tan thread, stitch inside the edges of the leaf shapes and in a swirling pattern on the berries as shown on the patterns to finish.

COMPLETING THE HOT MAT

Step 1. Press under ¼" around all sides of the prepared backing square.

Step 2. Lay the backing square right side down on a flat surface; center the batting square on the backing square.

Step 3. Center the finished block right side up on the layers; pin to hold in place.

Step 4. Bring opposite sides of the backing piece up and over the edges of the block as shown in Figure 4; press.

Figure 4

Step 5. Stitch close to the edge of the folded-over backing piece, again referring to Figure 4.

Step 6. Repeat Steps 4 and 5 on the remaining sides of the block, folding raw edges of ends in before stitching.

Step 7. Machine-stitch as in Step 7 of Completing the Topper to complete the hot mat. ❖

Holly Party Topper
Placement Diagram
30" x 30"

Holly Party Hot Mat
Placement Diagram
8½" x 8½"

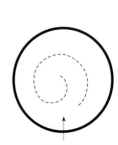

Berry
Cut 4 of each dark
red tonal for topper
Cut 1 of each dark
red tonal for hot mat

Holly Leaf
Cut 4 each medium & dark green tonals for topper
Cut 1 each medium & dark green tonals for hot mat

Poinsettia Table Set

Designs by **CHRIS MALONE**

Use the 3-D flowers to create matching napkin rings.

PROJECT SPECIFICATIONS
Skill Level: Intermediate
Runner Size: 42" x 15" without poinsettias
Napkin Size: 17" x 17"
Napkin Holder: 2" x 8" without poinsettia

MATERIALS
- 2 coordinating fat quarters for each napkin
- ⅛ yard each 1 red, 4 gold and 2 green fabrics for runner patchwork
- ⅛ yard each 7 red prints for poinsettia petals
- ⅝ yard green print for binding and napkin holder
- Backing 44½" x 17½"
- Needled polyester batting 44½" x 17½"
- Scraps batting
- All-purpose thread to match fabrics
- Quilting thread
- 8 (1⅛") covered button kits
- 1 (¾") covered button kit for each napkin holder
- 48 (6/0) gold glass beads
- 3 (6/0) gold glass beads for each napkin holder
- 1 size-3 snap for each napkin holder
- Permanent fabric glue
- Basic sewing tools and supplies

CUTTING
Step 1. Cut a total of (70) 3½" x 3½" squares from the assorted gold, green and red fabrics.

Step 2. Cut one 17½" x 17½" square from each of two fat quarters for each napkin.
Step 3. Cut 2¼"-wide bias strips green print and join with angled seams to make a piece of binding 120" long.
Step 4. Cut two 2½" x 8½" strips green print for each napkin holder.
Step 5. Cut one 2½" x 8½" strip batting scrap for each napkin holder.

COMPLETING THE RUNNER
Step 1. Arrange fabric squares in 14 rows of five squares each; join the squares to make rows. Press seams in adjoining rows in opposite directions. Join the rows to complete the pieced runner top.
Step 2. Use a plate as a pattern to round off each square corner of the pieced runner top.
Step 3. Quilt and bind using the prepared bias binding referring to Completing Your Quilt on page 173.

MAKING POINSETTIAS
Step 1. Prepare templates for the petal shapes using the patterns given.
Step 2. Trace eight large petals on the wrong side of each of the seven red prints, leaving ½" between petals.
Step 3. Fold the marked fabrics in half with right

sides facing and pin to scraps of batting with leaf shapes on top as shown in Figure 1.

Step 4. Sew on the marked lines around each petal shape through all layers, leaving bottom straight edge open, again referring to Figure 1.

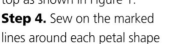

Figure 1

Step 5. Cut out stitched shapes, leaving a seam allowance around each one; trim batting close to seams. Clip points.

Step 6. Turn petals right side out; press.

Step 7. To assemble each flower, hand-gather along the bottom edge of one petal with a knotted double thread as shown in Figure 2.

Figure 2

Step 8. Add a second petal and gather. Continue to add petals until you have one petal of each fabric connected. Pull thread to gather and secure the end to the first petal, forming a circle of petals referring to Figure 3. Knot and clip thread; repeat to make eight large poinsettias.

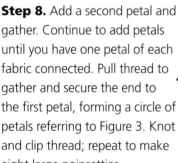

Figure 3

Step 9. Glue a scrap of batting to the top of each 1⅛" cover button; repeat with a piece of gold print. Add button backs referring to the manufacturer's instructions.

Step 10. Sew six gold glass beads to the center of each button as shown in Figure 4.

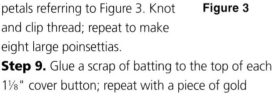

Figure 4

Step 11. For each poinsettia flower, place the shank of the button inside the center opening of a flower; add a small amount of permanent fabric glue to secure.

Step 12. Arrange four poinsettia flowers at each end of the runner referring to the Placement Diagram for positioning; tack shanks of buttons to the binding of the runner to hold in place. Secure with a few drops of permanent fabric glue to finish.

COMPLETING THE NAPKIN HOLDER

Step 1. To complete one napkin holder, refer to Making Poinsettias to complete one poinsettia flower using the small-petal pattern.

Step 2. Prepare a ¾" gold covered button and add three gold beads.

Step 3. Pin two 2½" x 8½" green print strips right sides together with same-size batting pieces; stitch all around, leaving a 2" opening on one side.

Step 4. Trim batting close to stitching; clip corners. Turn right side out and press.

Step 5. Turn the ¼" seam allowance in the opening to the inside; press. Hand-stitch closed.

Step 6. Topstitch ¼" from edge all around the edges of strip.

Step 7. Sew snap halves to ends of strip, one snap half on the inside and the opposite half on the outside so ends overlap and snap together as shown in Figure 5.

Figure 5 **Figure 6**

Step 8. Tack a small poinsettia flower to the right side of the holder at the end where the snap is

Poinsettia Napkin Holder
Placement Diagram
2" x 8" without poinsettia

Small Petal
Trace 1 on
each red print
for each
napkin holder

Large Petal
Trace 8 on
each red print
for runner

sewn to the wrong side as shown in Figure 6. Add a drop of permanent fabric glue to secure flower to holder to complete one napkin holder.

COMPLETING A NAPKIN

Step 1. Place two different 17½" x 17½" squares right sides together; stitch all around, leaving a 6" opening on one side.

Step 2. Clip corners and turn right side out through the opening; press.

Step 3. Turn the seam allowance in the opening to the inside; hand-stitch to close the opening.

Step 4. Topstitch ¼" from the edges all around to finish. ❖

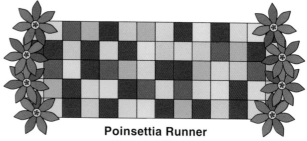

Poinsettia Runner
Placement Diagram
42" x 15" without poinsettias

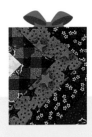
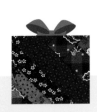
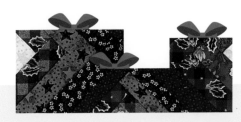

Christmas Log Runner

Design by **SANDRA L. HATCH**

Two sizes of Log Cabin blocks combine to make this large table runner

PROJECT SPECIFICATIONS

Skill Level: Beginner
Runner Size: 59" x 20¾"
Block Sizes: 12" x 12"
 and 7½" x 7½"
Number of Blocks: 3
 and 4

MATERIALS

- ¼ yard red holly check
- ¼ yard cream star tonal
- ⅓ yard dark red print
- ⅓ yard green print
- ⅓ yard green star tonal
- ⅝ yard green holly check
- ⅔ yard red print
- Backing 65" x 26"
- Batting 65" x 26"
- All-purpose thread to match fabrics
- Quilting thread
- Rotary rulers with 45- and 90-degree-angle marks
- Basic sewing tools and supplies

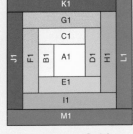

Large Log Cabin
12" x 12" Block
Make 3

Small Log Cabin
7½" x 7½" Block
Make 4

CUTTING

Step 1. Cut one 2" by fabric width strip red print; subcut strip into three each 3½" B1 and 5" C1 pieces.

Step 2. Cut one 1½" by fabric width strip red print; subcut strip into four each 2" B2 and 3" C2 pieces.

Step 3. Cut three 2⅜" by fabric width strips red print; subcut strips into eight 11¾" N pieces. Using the rotary ruler with 45-degree-angle mark, trim ends of each N piece at a 45-degree angle as shown in Figure 1.

45-degree-angle line

Figure 1

Step 4. Cut two 3⅜" by fabric width strips red print; subcut strips into two each 12½" P and 15⅜" Q strips.

Step 5. Cut two 2" by fabric width strips red holly check; subcut strips into three each 6½" F1 and 8" G1 pieces.

Step 6. Cut one 1½" by fabric width strip red holly check; subcut strip into four each 4" F2 and 5" G2 pieces.

Step 7. Cut two 2" by fabric width strips dark red print; subcut strips into three each 9½" J1 and 11" K1 pieces.

Step 8. Cut two 1½" by fabric width strips

dark red print; subcut strips into four each 6" J2 and 7" K2 pieces.

Step 9. Cut one 2" by fabric width strip green holly check; subcut strip into three each 5" D1 and 6½" E1 pieces.

Step 10. Cut one 1½" by fabric width strip green holly check; subcut strip into four each 3" D2 and 4" E2 pieces.

Step 11. Cut five 2¼" by fabric width strips green holly check for binding.

Step 12. Cut two 2" by fabric width strips green star tonal; subcut strips into three each 8" H1 and 9½" I1 strips.

Step 13. Cut two 1½" by fabric width strips

green star tonal; subcut strips into four each 5" H2 and 6" I2 pieces.

Step 14. Cut two 2" by fabric width strips green print; subcut strips into three each 11" L1 and 12½" M1 strips.

Step 15. Cut two 1½" by fabric width strips green print; subcut strips into four each 7" L2 and 8" M2 pieces.

Step 16. Cut one 5½" by fabric width strip cream star tonal; subcut strip into four 5½" squares. Cut each square in half on one diagonal to make eight O triangles. Cut the remainder of the strip into three 3½" x 3½" A1 squares and four 2" x 2" A2 squares.

COMPLETING THE BLOCKS

Step 1. To complete one Large Log Cabin block, sew B1 to A1; press seam toward B1.

Step 2. Add C1 to the A-B unit as shown in Figure 2; press seam toward C1.

Figure 2

Step 3. Continue adding lettered D1–M1 pieces around A1 in alphabetical order, pressing seams toward the newly added piece after stitching to complete one Large Log Cabin block referring to the block drawing. Repeat to make three Large Log Cabin blocks.

Step 4. Repeat Steps 1–3 to complete four Small Log Cabin blocks using A2–M2 pieces.

COMPLETING THE RUNNER

Step 1. Sew O to N as shown in Figure 3; press seam toward N. Repeat to make eight N-O units.

Figure 3

Figure 4

Step 2. Sew P to the M side of one Large Log Cabin block and to the K side of a second large block as shown in Figure 4; press seams toward P.

Step 3. Sew Q to the L side of the P/M block and to the J side of the P/K block as shown in Figure 5; press seams toward Q.

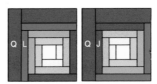

Figure 5

Step 4. Sew an N-O unit to the J and M sides of a Small Log Cabin block to make a side unit as shown in Figure 6; press seams toward the N-O units. Repeat to make four side units.

Figure 6   **Figure 7**

Step 5. Arrange the side units with the remaining unbordered large block and the two bordered large blocks in diagonal rows referring to Figure 7; join to make rows. Press seams in adjacent rows in opposite directions.

Step 6. Join the rows, stopping stitching at the end of the N/O seam as shown in Figure 8; press seams in one direction. **Note:** *The angled ends of the center N pieces will be unstitched at this point.*

Figure 8   **Figure 9**   **Figure 10**

Step 7. Fold the pieced top in half with the unstitched angled ends right sides together as shown in Figure 9. Place ruler, matching ¼" line with N/O seam intersection referring to Figure 10.

Step 8. Starting at inside edge of N, cut to make a 90-degree angle, again referring to Figure 10. Repeat on the opposite side of the runner.

Step 9. Stitch ¼" from cut edge and press seam open as shown in Figure 11. Repeat on both sides to complete a straight side on each side center as shown in Figure 12.

Figure 11   **Figure 12**

Step 10. Quilt and bind referring to Completing Your Quilt on page 173. ❖

Christmas Log Runner
Placement Diagram
59" x 20¾"

All Wrapped Up

Design by **JULIE WEAVER**

Fabric placement in the blocks creates the look of a wrapped Christmas package.

PROJECT SPECIFICATIONS

Skill Level: Beginner
Runner Size:
 38½" x 16½"
Block Size: 10" x 10"
Number of Blocks: 3

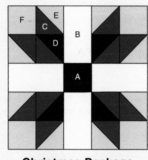

Christmas Package
10" x 10" Block

MATERIALS

- ¼ yard tan mottled
- ¼ yard green print
- ⅓ yard cream holly print
- ⅞ yard red tonal
- Backing 44" x 22"
- Batting 44" x 22"
- All-purpose thread to match fabrics
- Quilting thread
- Basic sewing tools and supplies

CUTTING

Step 1. Cut one 2⅞" by fabric width strip green print; subcut strip into six 2⅞" squares for D. Trim the remainder of the strip to 2½" and subcut into three 2½" A squares.

Step 2. Cut one 2" by fabric width strip green print; subcut strip into four 2" L squares. Trim the remainder of the strip to 1½" and subcut eight 1½" H squares. Trim the remainder of the strip to 1¼" and cut into four 1¼" I squares.

Step 3. Cut two 2⅞" by fabric width strips red tonal; subcut strips into (18) 2⅞" C squares.

Step 4. Cut one 10½" by fabric width strip red tonal; subcut strip into (10) 1½" G strips. Trim the remainder of the strip into two 2" x 14" M strips.

Step 5. Cut two 2" x 36" N strips red tonal.

Step 6. Cut three 2¼" by fabric width strips red tonal for binding.

Step 7. Cut one 4½" by fabric width strip cream holly print; subcut strip into (12) 2½" B rectangles.

Step 8. Cut three 1¼" by fabric width strips cream holly print; subcut one strip into two 12½" J strips. Trim the remaining strips to make two 34½" K strips.

Step 9. Cut one 2½" by fabric width strip tan mottled; subcut strip into (12) 2½" F squares.

Step 10. Cut one 2⅞" by fabric width strip tan mottled; subcut strip into (12) 2⅞" E squares.

ALL WRAPPED UP

COMPLETING THE BLOCKS

Step 1. Draw a diagonal line from corner to corner on the wrong side of each C square.

Step 2. Place a C square right sides together with a D square; stitch ¼" on each side of the marked line as shown in Figure 1.

Figure 1   **Figure 2**

Step 3. Cut the C-D unit in half on the marked line as shown in Figure 2; open and press seam toward C to complete two C-D units. Repeat to make 12 C-D units.

Step 4. Repeat Steps 2 and 3 with C and E squares to complete 24 C-E units as shown in Figure 3.

Figure 3   **Figure 4**

Step 5. To complete one block, join one each C-D and C-E unit as shown in Figure 4; press seam toward the C-D unit.

Step 6. Sew F to one C-E unit as shown in Figure 5; press seam toward F.

Figure 5

Step 7. Join the C-D-E unit with the C-E-F unit to complete one corner unit as shown in Figure 6; press seam toward the C-E-F unit. Repeat to make four corner units.

Figure 6   **Figure 7**

Step 8. Join two corner units with B as shown in Figure 7 to make a B row; press seams toward B. Repeat to make two B rows.

All Wrapped Up
Placement Diagram
38½" x 16½"

Step 9. Sew A between two B pieces to make the center row as shown in Figure 8; press seams toward B.

Step 10. Sew the center row between the two B rows as shown in Figure 8 to complete one Christmas Package block; press seams toward the center row. Repeat to make three blocks.

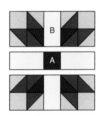

Figure 8

COMPLETING THE RUNNER

Step 1. Join the three pieced blocks with four G strips to complete the pieced center; press seams toward G strips.

Step 2. Join three G strips with four H squares to make a sashing strip; press seams toward H. Repeat to make two sashing strips.

Step 3. Sew a sashing strip to opposite sides of the pieced center; press seams toward sashing strips.

Step 4. Sew K to opposite long sides of the pieced center; press seams toward K.

Step 5. Sew an I square to each end of each J strip; press seams toward J strips. Sew an I/J strip to opposite short ends of the pieced center; press seams toward I/J strips.

Step 6. Sew N to opposite long sides of the pieced center; press seams toward N.

Step 7. Sew an L square to each end of each M strip; press seams toward M strips. Sew an L/M strip to opposite short ends of the pieced center; press seams toward L/M strips to complete the pieced top.

Step 8. Quilt and bind referring to Completing Your Quilt on page 173. ❖

Christmas Squares

Design by **JULIE WEAVER**

Use your favorite Christmas prints to stitch a holiday runner.

PROJECT SPECIFICATIONS
Skill Level:
   Intermediate
Runner Size:
   $50\frac{5}{8}$" x 16"
Block Size: 9" x 9"
Number of Blocks: 3

Christmas Squares
9" x 9" Block

MATERIALS
- $\frac{3}{8}$ yard cream print
- $\frac{5}{8}$ yard green print
- 1 yard red print
- Backing 57" x 22"
- Batting 57" x 22"
- All-purpose thread to match fabrics
- Quilting thread
- Basic sewing tools and supplies

CUTTING
Step 1. Cut one 1½" by fabric width strip red print; subcut strip into five 1½" A squares.
Step 2. Cut one 5¼" by fabric width strip red print; cut one 5¼" G square from the strip. Trim strip to 4⅞"; subcut strip into six 4⅞" squares for C.
Step 3. Cut four 2½" by fabric width strips red print; set aside two strips for N. Cut each of the

remaining strips in half to make four 21"-long strips for O and P.
Step 4. Cut five 2½" by fabric width strips red print for binding.
Step 5. Cut one 5¼" by fabric width strip green print; subcut strip into three 5¼" D squares.
Step 6. Cut one 4½" by fabric width strip green print; subcut strip into (14) 1½" B rectangles.
Step 7. Cut one 1½" by fabric width strip green print; subcut strip into four 9½" F strips.
Step 8. Cut four 1½" by fabric width strips green print; set aside two strips for H. Cut each of the remaining strips in half to make four 21"-long strips for I and J.
Step 9. Cut one 5¼" by fabric width strip cream print; subcut strip into four 5¼" E squares.
Step 10. Cut four 1" by fabric width strips cream print; set aside two strips for K. Cut each of the remaining strips in half to make four 21"-long strips for L and M.

COMPLETING THE BLOCKS
Step 1. Draw a diagonal line from corner to corner on the wrong side of each E square.
Step 2. Place an E square right sides together with each D square; stitch ¼" on each side of the marked line as shown in Figure 1.

Step 3. Cut stitched units apart on the marked line and press open with seam toward D, again referring to Figure 1.

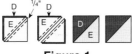

Figure 1

Step 4. Draw a diagonal line from corner to corner on the wrong side of the D-E units as shown in Figure 2.

Step 5. Place the marked D-E units right sides together with the C squares; stitch ¼" on each side of the marked line as shown in Figure 3.

Figure 2

Figure 3

Step 6. Cut apart on the marked line and press open with seam toward C to complete six each C-D-E and reversed C-D-E units as shown in Figure 4.

Reversed
Make 6   Make 6

Figure 4

CHRISTMAS SQUARES RUNNER

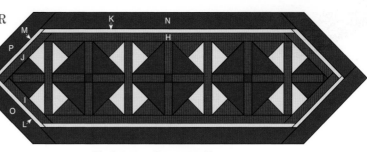

Christmas Squares Runner
Placement Diagram
50⅝" x 16"

Step 7. To complete one block, join one each C-D-E and reversed C-D-E unit with B to make the top row as shown in Figure 5; press seams toward B. Repeat to make the bottom row.

Step 8. Sew A between two B pieces to make an A-B unit; press seams toward A.

Figure 5

Figure 6

Step 9. Join the top and bottom rows with the A-B unit to complete one block as shown in Figure 6; press seams toward the A-B unit. Repeat to make three blocks.

COMPLETING THE RUNNER

Step 1. Place the remaining E square right sides together with G; stitch ¼" on each side of the marked line as shown in Figure 7.

Figure 7

Step 2. Cut apart on the marked line to complete two E-G units, again referring to Figure 7; open and press seams toward G.

Step 3. Cut each E-G unit in half on one diagonal to make two each E-G and reversed E-G units as shown in Figure 8.

Figure 8

Figure 9

Step 4. Join one each E-G and reversed E-G units with B and add A as shown in Figure 9; press seams toward B.

Step 5. Trim excess A even with the E-G angle to complete one corner unit, again referring to Figure 9; repeat to make two corner units.

Step 6. Join the blocks and corner units with F strips to complete the pieced center referring to Figure 10; press seams toward F strips.

Figure 10

Step 7. Center and sew an H strip to opposite long sides of the pieced center; press seams toward H strips. Trim each end of each H strip even with angle at the ends of the pieced center as shown in Figure 11.

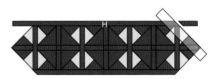

Figure 11

Step 8. Sew an I strip to opposite ends of the pieced center, press seams toward the I strips and trim as in Step 7 referring to Figure 12.

Figure 12

Step 9. Continue adding, pressing and trimming strips in alphabetical order referring to the Placement Diagram to complete the pieced top.

Step 10. Quilt and bind referring to Completing Your Quilt on page 173. ❖

Gingerbear Boys

Design by **JULIE HIGGINS**

This fun quilt looks good on a table or the wall.

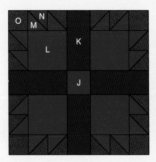

Bear Paw
9" x 9" Block
Make 1

Teddy Bear
9" x 9" Block
Make 4

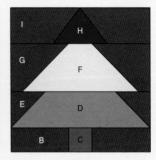

Tree
9" x 9" Block
Make 4

PROJECT SPECIFICATIONS
Skill Level: Intermediate
Quilt Size: 38" x 38"
Block Size: 9" x 9"
Number of Blocks: 9

MATERIALS
- 4" x 8" scrap white tonal
- ⅛ yard each green/white stripe, green check and green print
- ⅓ yard rust mottled
- ¾ yard black holly print
- ¾ yard red print
- ⅞ yard black solid
- Backing 44" x 44"
- Batting 44" x 44"
- All-purpose thread to match fabrics
- Quilting thread
- 4 (½") black buttons
- 8 (⅜") black buttons
- 12 (¼") assorted-color buttons
- 12 assorted-color star buttons
- ½ yard fusible web
- Basic sewing tools and supplies

CUTTING
Step 1. Cut one 9½" by fabric width strip black solid; subcut strip into four 9½" A squares. Fold and crease each square on both diagonals to mark the diagonal centers.

Step 2. Cut one 2" by fabric width strip black solid; subcut strip into eight 4¼" B rectangles.

Step 3. Cut two 2¾" by fabric width strips black solid; subcut strips into eight 2¾" E squares.

Step 4. Cut one 3½" by fabric width strip black solid; subcut strip into eight 4¼" G rectangles.

Step 5. Cut one 2⅛" by fabric width strip black solid; subcut strip into eight 2⅛" N squares. Trim remainder of strip to 1¾"; subcut into four 1¾" O squares.

Step 6. Cut four 2¾" x 9½" D rectangles green check.

Step 7. Cut four 3½" x 8" F rectangles green/white stripe.

Step 8. Cut four 2" x 4¼" K rectangles green print.

GINGERBEAR BOYS

Step 9. Cut one 2⅛" by fabric width strip red print; subcut strip into eight 2⅛" M squares and one 2" x 2" J square.

Step 10. Cut four 3" x 3" L squares red print.

Step 11. Cut two 1½" x 27½" P strips and two 1½" x 29½" Q strips red print.

Step 12. Cut four 2¼" by fabric width strips red print for binding.

Step 13. Cut two 5" x 29½" R strips and two 5" x 38½" S strips black holly print.

Step 14. Cut four 2" x 2" C squares rust mottled.

Step 15. Prepare templates for H and I pieces using patterns given; cut as directed on each piece.

COMPLETING THE TEDDY BEAR BLOCKS

Step 1. Trace the teddy bear shapes onto the paper side of the fusible web referring to pattern for number to cut; cut out shapes, leaving a margin around each one.

Step 2. Fuse the teddy bear shapes to the wrong side of the rust mottled and the muzzle shapes to the wrong side of the white tonal. Cut out shapes on traced lines; remove paper backing.

Step 3. Arrange and fuse the muzzle shapes to the teddy bear shapes referring to pattern for placement.

Step 4. Center and fuse a teddy bear shape on each A square using diagonal crease lines on A and center mark on pattern as guides for placement.

Step 5. Using black thread and a medium-width, close zigzag stitch, stitch around each bear and muzzle shape to complete the blocks. **Note:** *Buttons are added after quilting is complete.*

COMPLETING THE TREE BLOCKS

Step 1. Sew I and IR to opposite sides of H to complete an H-I unit as shown in Figure 1; press seams toward I and IR. Repeat to make four H-I units.

Figure 1

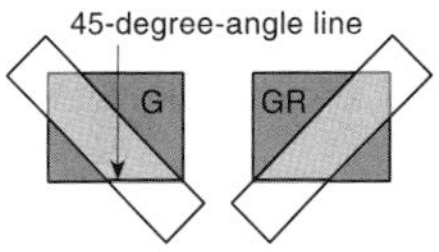

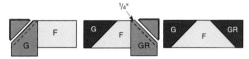

45-degree-angle line

Figure 2

Step 2. Mark a 45-degree-angle line on the wrong side of each G rectangle to make four and four reversed G rectangles as shown in Figure 2.

Step 3. Place a marked G piece right sides together with F, matching the straight edges as shown in Figure 3; stitch on the marked line, trim and press as in Step 1. Repeat with a reversed G piece to complete one F-G unit, again referring to Figure 3. Repeat to complete four F-G units.

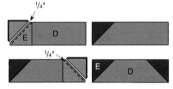

Figure 3

Step 4. Mark a diagonal line from corner to corner on the wrong side of each E piece.

Step 5. Stitch an E piece to each end of D to complete four D-E units referring to Figure 4.

Figure 4

Step 6. Sew C between two B rectangles to complete a B-C unit as shown in Figure 5; press seams toward B. Repeat to make four B-C units.

Figure 5

Step 7. Arrange the pieced units as shown in Figure 6 and join to complete one Tree block; press seams in one direction. Repeat to make four blocks.

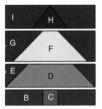

Figure 6

COMPLETING THE BEAR PAW BLOCK

Step 1. Mark a diagonal line from corner to corner on the wrong side of each M square.

Step 2. Place an M square right sides together with an N square; stitch ¼" on each side of the marked line referring to Figure 7. Repeat for all N-M squares.

Figure 7

Figure 8

Step 3. Cut stitched units apart on marked lines and press seams toward N to complete 16 M-N units as shown in Figure 8.

Step 4. Join two M-N units as shown in Figure 9; press seam in one direction. Repeat to make four M-N and four reversed M-N units, again referring to Figure 9.

Make 4   Reverse
            Make 4

Figure 9

Figure 10

Step 5. Sew O to the N side of the M-N units as shown in Figure 10; press seams toward O.

Step 6. Sew a reversed M-N unit to one side and an M-N-O unit to the adjacent side of L to make a corner unit as shown in Figure 11; press seams toward L. Repeat to make four corner units.

Figure 11   **Figure 12**

Step 7. Join two corner units with K to make a block row as shown in Figure 12; press seams toward K. Repeat to make two block rows.

Step 8. Join two K rectangles with J; press seams toward J.

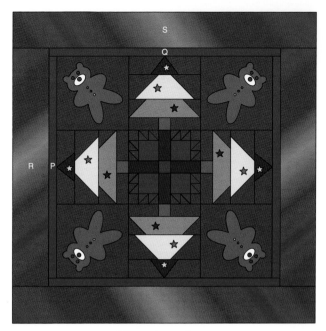

GIngerbear Boys
Placement Diagram
38" x 38"

Step 9. Join the two block rows with the J-K unit to complete the Bear Paw block as shown in Figure 13; press seams toward the J-K unit.

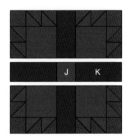

Figure 13

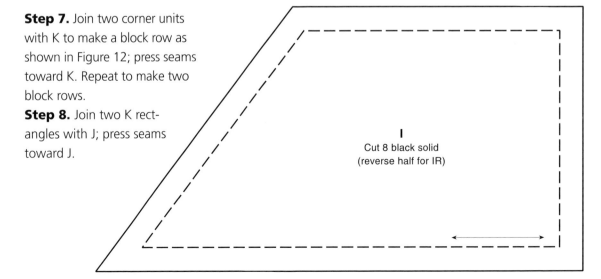

I
Cut 8 black solid
(reverse half for IR)

COMPLETING THE QUILT

Step 1. Sew a Tree block between two Teddy Bear blocks to make a bear row referring to the Placement Diagram for positioning of blocks; repeat to make two bear rows. Press seams toward the Tree block.

Step 2. Sew the Bear Paw block between two Tree blocks to make the center row, again referring to the Placement Diagram for positioning of blocks. Press seams toward the Tree blocks.

Step 3. Join the rows referring to the Placement Diagram for positioning; press seams away from the center row.

Step 4. Sew P strips to opposite sides and Q strips to the top and bottom of the pieced center; press seams toward the P and Q strips.

Step 5. Sew R strips to opposite sides and S strips to the top and bottom of the pieced center; press seams toward the R and S strips.

Step 6. Quilt and bind referring to Completing Your Quilt on page 173.

Step 7. Sew a ½" black button to each muzzle area for nose.

Step 8. Sew two ⅜" black buttons to each teddy bear shape for eyes.

Step 9. Sew three ¼" buttons to teddy bear shapes as marked on pattern.

Step 10. Sew a star button to each D, F and H piece referring to the Placement Diagram for positioning suggestions to complete the quilt. ❖

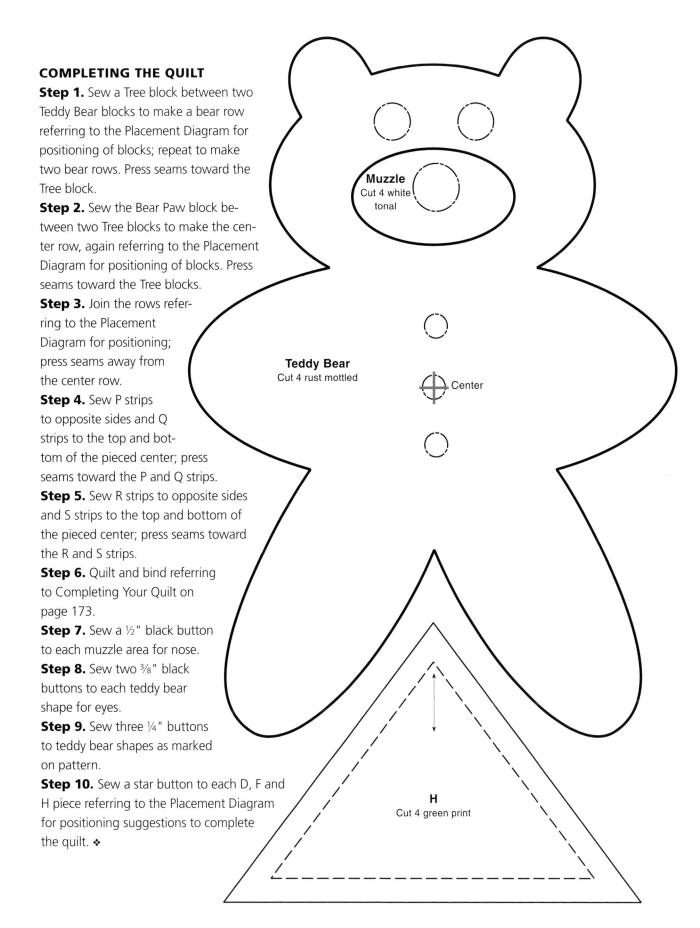

Muzzle
Cut 4 white tonal

Teddy Bear
Cut 4 rust mottled

Center

H
Cut 4 green print

Jolly Old St. Nick

Design by **JULIE WEAVER**

Combine piecing and appliqué to make the blocks in this holiday wall quilt.

PROJECT SPECIFICATIONS

Skill Level: Beginner
Quilt Size: 19" x 32"
Block Size: 6" x 8"
Number of Blocks: 6

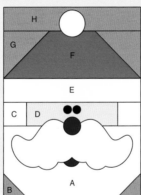

Jolly Old St. Nick
6" x 8" Block

MATERIALS

- 6 different 3" x 9" white/cream tonals (hat brims and pompoms)
- 6 different 7" x 12" white/cream prints (beards and mustaches)
- 6 different 4" x 9" red/burgundy tonals (hats)
- ⅛ yard tan solid
- ¼ yard burgundy tonal
- ¼ yard blue tonal
- ⅝ yard green print
- Backing 25" x 38"
- Batting 25" x 38"
- All-purpose thread to match fabrics and black
- Quilting thread
- 12 (½") black buttons
- ¼ yard fusible web
- Basic sewing tools and supplies

CUTTING

Step 1. Cut one 3½" x 6½" A rectangle and two 1½" x 1½" C squares from each 7" x 12" white/cream print rectangle.

Step 2. Cut one 1½" x 6½" E piece from each 3" x 9" white/cream tonal rectangle.

Step 3. Cut one 2½" x 6½" F piece from each 4" x 9" red/burgundy tonal rectangle.

Step 4. Cut one 1½" by fabric width strip tan solid; subcut strip into six 4½" D pieces.

Step 5. Cut two 1½" by fabric width strips blue tonal; subcut strips into (12) 1½" B squares and six 6½" H rectangles. Mark a diagonal line from corner to corner on the wrong side of each B square.

Step 6. Cut one 2½" by fabric width strip blue tonal; subcut strip into (12) 2½" G squares. Mark a diagonal line from corner to corner on the wrong side of each square.

Step 7. Cut four 1½" by fabric width strips burgundy tonal; subcut strips into three 8½" I and two each 13½" J, 26½" K and 15½" L strips.

Step 8. Cut three 2½" by fabric width strips green print for binding.

Step 9. Cut three 2½" by fabric width strips green print; subcut strips into two 28½" M strips and two 19½" N strips.

Step 10. Trace appliqué motifs onto the paper side of the fusible web as directed on pattern pieces for number to cut; cut out shapes, leaving a margin around each one.

Step 11. Fuse shapes to the wrong side of the fabric rectangles and burgundy tonal as directed on patterns for color; cut out shapes on traced lines. Remove paper backing.

COMPLETING THE BLOCKS

Step 1. Place two B squares right sides together on the corners of A and stitch on the marked line as shown in Figure 1; trim seam to ¼" and press B to the right side to complete an A-B unit. Repeat to make six A-B units.

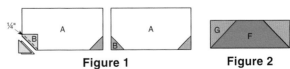

Figure 1   Figure 2

Step 2. Sew two matching C squares to the ends of D; press seams toward C. Repeat to make six C-D units.

Step 3. Repeat Step 1 with two G squares on F as shown in Figure 2.

Step 4. Join the pieced units with E and H as shown in Figure 3 to complete the block piecing.

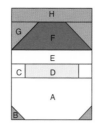

Figure 3

Step 5. Arrange and fuse the appliqué shapes on each pieced block referring to the block drawing.

Step 6. Using black all-purpose thread and a medium-width machine buttonhole stitch, stitch around edges of the appliqué shapes.

Step 7. To complete each block, sew two ½" black buttons in place on the D piece above the nose to make eyes, referring to the block drawing for positioning.

COMPLETING THE QUILT

Step 1. Join two blocks with one I strip to make a row referring to Figure 4; press seams toward the I strips. Repeat to make three rows.

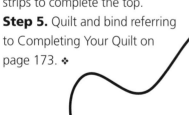

Figure 4

Step 2. Join the rows with the J strips to complete the pieced center; press seams toward the J strips.

Step 3. Sew K strips to opposite long sides and L strips to the top and bottom of the pieced center; press seams toward K and L strips.

Step 4. Sew the M strips to opposite long sides and N strips to the top and bottom of the pieced center; press seams toward M and N strips to complete the top.

Step 5. Quilt and bind referring to Completing Your Quilt on page 173. ❖

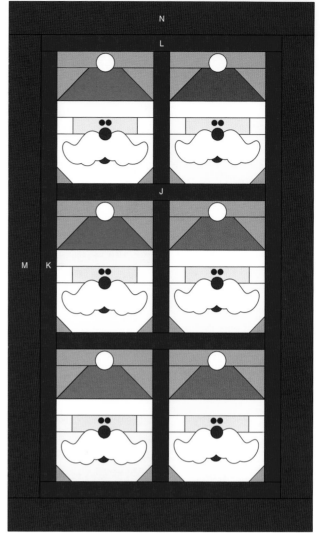

Jolly Old St. Nick
Placement Diagram
19" x 32"

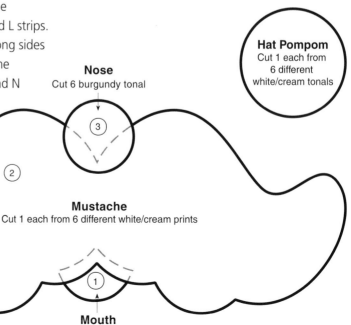

Nose
Cut 6 burgundy tonal

Hat Pompom
Cut 1 each from 6 different white/cream tonals

Mustache
Cut 1 each from 6 different white/cream prints

Mouth
Cut 6 burgundy tonal

Ho, Ho, Ho Wall Quilt

Design by **JULIE WEAVER**

Santa makes a statement in this seasonal wall quilt.

PROJECT SPECIFICATIONS
Skill Level: Intermediate
Quilt Size: 28" x 40"

MATERIALS
- 3" x 6" rectangle tan solid
- ⅛ yard white tonal (hat trim, pompom and sleeve trim)
- ⅛ yard black tonal
- ¼ yard cream tonal (beard and mustache)
- ¼ yard burgundy mottled
- ½ yard red tonal
- 1 yard green print
- 1 yard tan tonal
- Backing 34" x 46"
- Batting 34" x 46"
- All-purpose thread to match fabrics and black
- Quilting thread
- ¾ yard fusible web
- Basic sewing tools and supplies

CUTTING
Step 1. Cut one 12½" by fabric width strip tan tonal; subcut strip into one 12½" A square and one 24½" K rectangle.
Step 2. Cut three 2⅞" by fabric width strips each tan tonal (B) and green print (C); subcut strips into (32) 2⅞" squares each for B and C. Mark a diagonal line from corner to corner on the wrong side of each B square.

Step 3. Cut one 2½" by fabric width strip tan tonal; subcut strip into eight 2½" D squares.
Step 4. Cut four 1¼" by fabric width strips tan tonal; subcut strips into two strips each in the following sizes: 16½" E; 18" F; 19" I; and 20½" J.
Step 5. Cut six 1" by fabric width strips red tonal; subcut strips into two strips each in the following sizes: 18" G; 19" H; 36½" L; and 25½" M.
Step 6. Cut four 2" by fabric width strips green print; subcut strips into two 37½" N strips and two 28½" O strips.
Step 7. Cut four 2½" by fabric width strips green print for binding.
Step 8. Trace each appliqué shape onto the paper side of the fusible web referring to the patterns for number to cut; cut out shapes, leaving a margin around each one.
Step 9. Fuse paper shapes to the wrong side of fabrics as directed on each piece for color; cut out shapes on traced lines. Remove paper backing.

COMPLETING THE QUILT
Step 1. Place a B square right sides together with a C square; stitch ¼" on each side of the marked line as shown in Figure 1.

Figure 1

Figure 2

Step 2. Cut apart on the marked line, open and press seam toward C to complete two B-C units as shown in Figure 2. Repeat to make 64 B-C units.

Step 3. Join three B-C units to make a B-C strip as shown in Figure 3; press seams in one direction. Repeat to make four each B-C and reversed B-C strips.

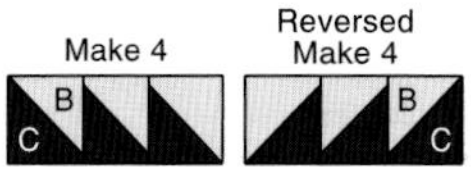

Figure 3

Step 4. Join a B-C strip and reversed B-C strip as shown in Figure 4; press seam in one direction. Repeat to make four strips.

Figure 4

Step 5. Sew a strip to opposite sides of A as shown in Figure 5; press seams toward A.

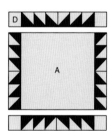

Figure 5

Step 6. Sew a D square to each end of the remaining joined B-C strips; press seams toward D.

Step 7. Sew the B-C-D strips to the remaining sides of A, again referring to Figure 5; press seams toward A.

Step 8. Sew E strips to opposite sides and F strips to the top and bottom of the pieced center; press seams toward the E and F strips.

Step 9. Repeat Step 8 with the G, H, I and J strips, pressing seams away from each newly added strip before adding the next strip.

Step 10. Join five B-C units as shown in Figure 6; press seams in one direction. Repeat to make four each B-C and reversed B-C strips.

Figure 6

Step 11. Join a B-C and reversed B-C strip to make a strip as shown in Figure 7; press seam in one direction. Repeat to make four strips.

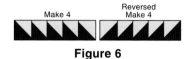

Figure 7

Step 12. Sew a strip to opposite sides of the pieced center; press seams toward I.

Step 13. Sew a D square to each end of the remaining two strips; press seams toward D.

Step 14. Sew the B-C-D strips to the top and bottom of the pieced center; press seams toward J.

Step 15. Sew K to the bottom of the pieced center; press seam toward K.

Step 16. Sew L strips to opposite long sides and M strips to the top and bottom of the pieced center; press seams toward L and M strips.

Step 17. Sew N strips to opposite long sides and O strips to the top and bottom of the pieced center to complete the pieced top; press seams toward the N and O strips.

Step 18. Fold and crease the A area of the pieced top to mark the center.

Step 19. Center, arrange and fuse the Santa appliqué pieces in numerical order on A referring to the full-size pattern and the Placement Diagram for positioning.

Step 20. Arrange and fuse the "HO HO HO" message and holly leaf and berries on the K area referring to the Placement Diagram for positioning.

Step 21. Using black all-purpose thread and a machine buttonhole stitch, stitch around each fused shape to complete the top.

Step 22. Quilt and bind referring to Completing Your Quilt on page 173. ❖

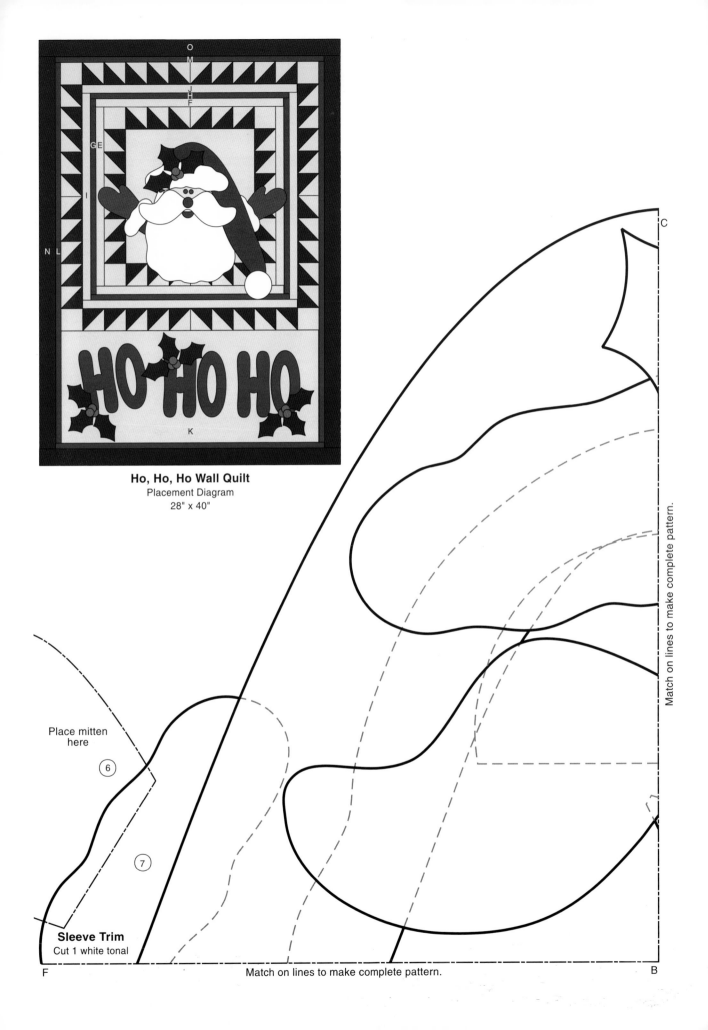

Ho, Ho, Ho Wall Quilt
Placement Diagram
28" x 40"

Place mitten here

⑥

⑦

Sleeve Trim
Cut 1 white tonal

Match on lines to make complete pattern.

Match on lines to make complete pattern.

F

B

C

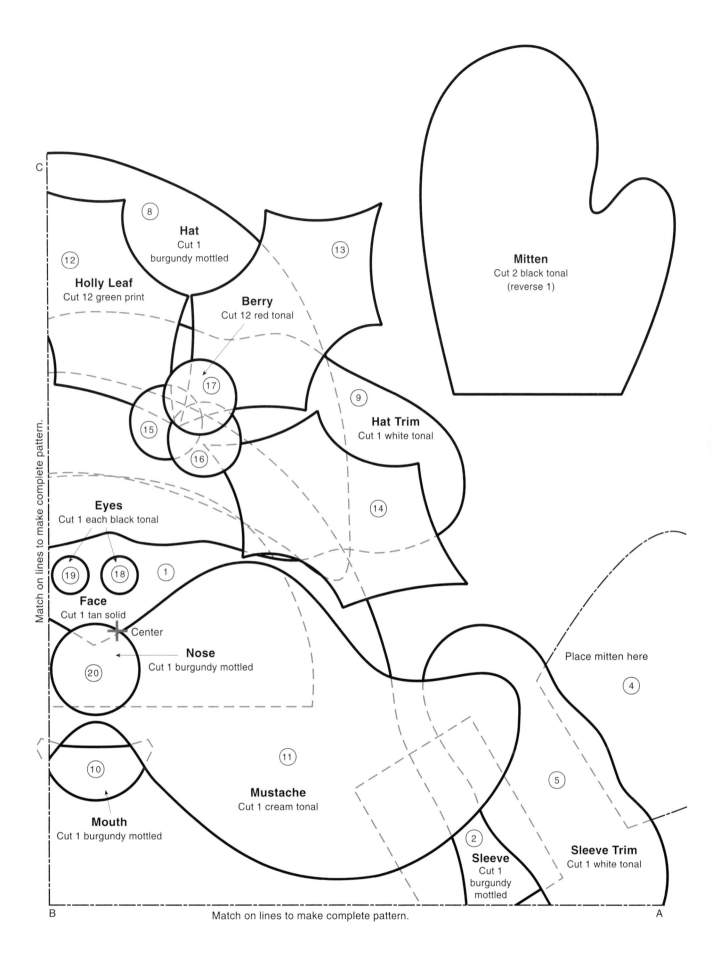

C

(8)

Hat
Cut 1
burgundy mottled

(13)

(12)

Holly Leaf
Cut 12 green print

Berry
Cut 12 red tonal

Mitten
Cut 2 black tonal
(reverse 1)

(17)

(15)

(9)

(16)

Hat Trim
Cut 1 white tonal

(14)

Match on lines to make complete pattern.

Eyes
Cut 1 each black tonal

(19) (18) (1)

Face
Cut 1 tan solid

Center

Nose
Cut 1 burgundy mottled

(20)

Place mitten here

(4)

(10)

(11)

Mustache
Cut 1 cream tonal

(5)

Mouth
Cut 1 burgundy mottled

(2)

Sleeve
Cut 1
burgundy
mottled

Sleeve Trim
Cut 1 white tonal

B

Match on lines to make complete pattern.

A

HO, HO, HO WALL QUILT

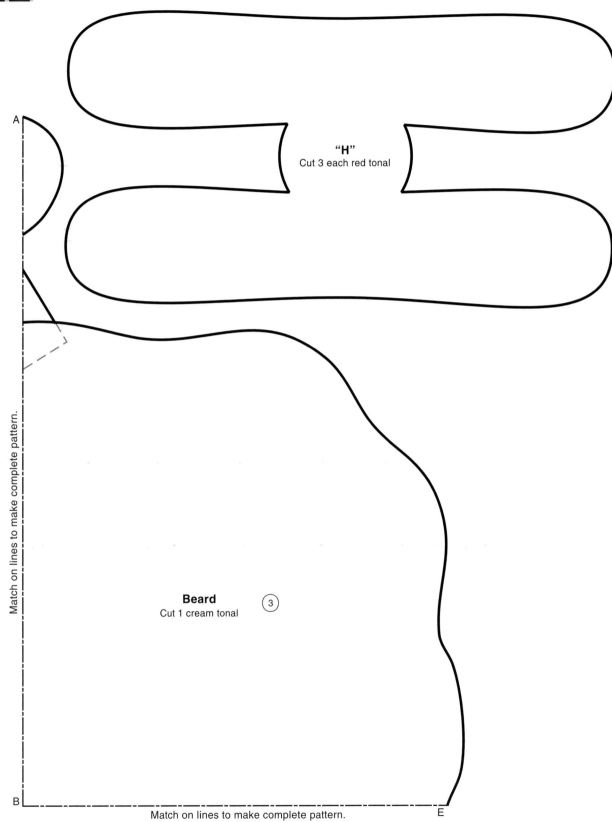

"H"
Cut 3 each red tonal

A

B

E

Match on lines to make complete pattern.

Match on lines to make complete pattern.

Beard
Cut 1 cream tonal ③

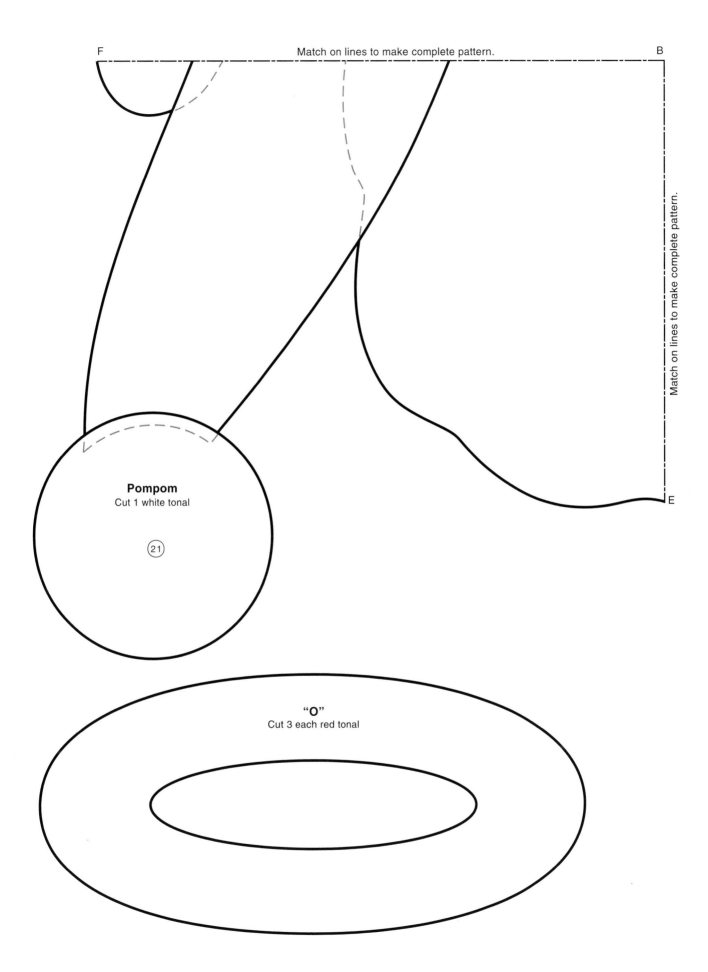

F

B

Match on lines to make complete pattern.

E

Pompom
Cut 1 white tonal

(21)

"O"
Cut 3 each red tonal

First Snow

Design by **CHRIS MALONE**

Add a bit of fun by sewing buttons on your quilt.

PROJECT SPECIFICATIONS
Skill Level: Beginner
Quilt Size: 17" x 17"

MATERIALS
- Scraps of 8 assorted green fabrics
- Scrap brown tonal
- 2" x 12" scrap white tonal
- ¼ yard green-with-blue dot
- ½ yard blue dot tonal
- Backing 17½" x 17½"
- Batting 17½" x 17½"
- All-purpose thread to match fabrics
- White hand-quilting thread
- ½ yard fusible web
- 28 assorted ⅜"–⅝" white buttons
- 2 (1") plastic rings
- Basic sewing tools and supplies

CUTTING
Step 1. Cut one 11½" x 11½" A square blue dot tonal.

Step 2. Cut two 1" x 16½" D strips and two 1" x 17½" E strips blue dot tonal.

Step 3. Cut two 3" x 11½" B strips and two 3" x 16½" C strips green-with-blue dots.

Step 4. Trace appliqué shapes given onto the paper side of the fusible web referring to the patterns for number to cut; cut out shapes, leaving a margin around each one.

Step 5. Fuse shapes to the wrong side of the assorted scraps as directed on patterns for color and number to cut; cut out shapes on traced lines. Remove paper backing.

COMPLETING THE QUILT
Step 1. Arrange and fuse appliqué shapes on A referring to Figure 1 for positioning and order of placement. ***Note:*** *Snow piece extends only ⅛" into the seam allowance of A as shown in Figure 1.*

Figure 1

Step 2. Sew B strips to opposite sides and C strips to the top and bottom of the appliquéd center; press seams toward B and C strips.

Step 3. Sew D strips to opposite sides and E strips to the top and bottom of the pieced center; press seams toward D and E strips.

Step 4. Place the backing square right side up on the batting square. Place the completed top right sides together with the layered backing and batting; stitch all around, leaving a 4" opening on one side.

Step 5. Clip corners; trim batting close to stitching line. Turn right side out through the opening.

Step 6. Turn raw edges of opening ¼" to the inside and press; hand-stitch opening closed. Press the edges flat.

FIRST SNOW

Step 7. Arrange buttons along the top of the snow piece and hand-stitch in place.

Step 8. Arrange seven buttons on A referring to the Placement Diagram for positioning suggestions; hand-stitch in place.

Step 9. Using white hand-quilting thread, stitch concentric circles around each button in the A area referring to the project photo.

Step 10. Sew a 1" plastic ring to the top back corners to finish. ❖

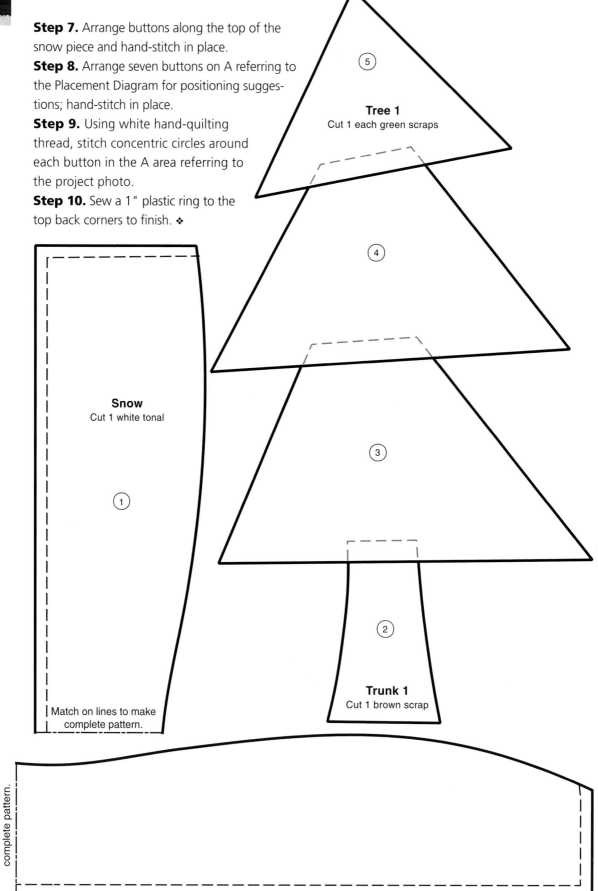

Tree 1
Cut 1 each green scraps

⑤

④

③

Snow
Cut 1 white tonal

①

Match on lines to make
complete pattern.

②

Trunk 1
Cut 1 brown scrap

Match on lines to make complete pattern.

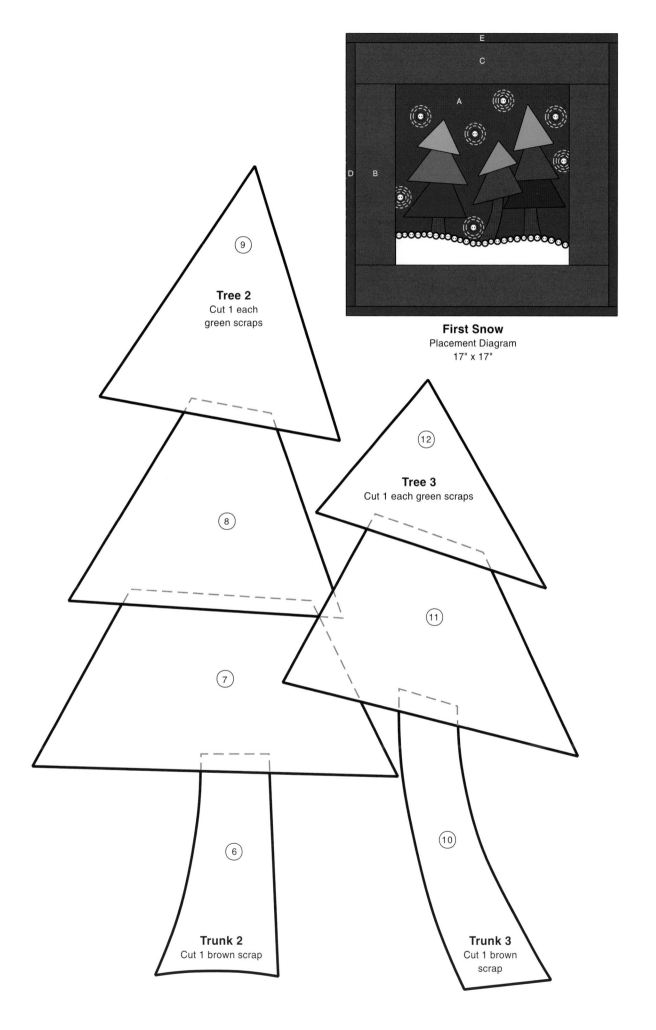

First Snow
Placement Diagram
17" x 17"

9

Tree 2
Cut 1 each
green scraps

8

7

6

Trunk 2
Cut 1 brown scrap

12

Tree 3
Cut 1 each green scraps

11

10

Trunk 3
Cut 1 brown
scrap

Christmas Kitty

Design by **CONNIE RAND**

The kitty is enjoying the Christmas tree,
not noticing that his little mouse neighbor
has put up a tree of his own!

PROJECT SPECIFICATIONS
Skill Level: Beginner
Quilt Size: 20½" x 20½"

MATERIALS
- Scraps red, yellow, blue, white, brown, black and green solids or tonals
- 1 fat quarter each dark green tonal, red print and diagonal Christmas stripe
- 9¾" x 12" A rectangle gold metallic
- 2¾" x 12" B rectangle brown-and-green horizontal stripe
- ¼ yard red solid
- Backing 24" x 24"
- Batting 24" x 24"
- All-purpose thread to match fabrics
- Quilting thread
- ¼ yard fusible web
- ⅓ yard fabric stabilizer
- 9 each ⅜" red and gold jingle bells
- 3 small flower spangles
- 1 small gold tree spangle
- 2 (4mm) wiggly eyes
- Fabric glue
- Basic sewing tools and supplies

CUTTING
Step 1. Cut four 1½" x 12" C strips, four 2" x 2" E squares and four 3½" x 3½" G squares red print.

Step 2. Cut four 2" x 12" D strips dark green tonal.

Step 3. Cut four 3½" x 15" F strips diagonal Christmas stripe.

Step 4. Cut three 2¼" by fabric width strips red solid for binding.

Step 5. Trace appliqué patterns onto paper side of fusible web referring to patterns for number to cut.

Step 6. Cut out shapes, leaving a margin around each one.

Step 7. Fuse shapes to the wrong side of fabrics as directed on each piece for color and number to cut; remove paper backing.

COMPLETING THE QUILT

Step 1. Sew A to B along the 12" edges referring to Figure 1.

Figure 1

Step 2. Arrange the appliqué pieces on the A-B background in numerical order referring to the Placement Diagram for positioning. When satisfied with arrangement, fuse shapes in place.

Step 3. Place fabric stablizer behind the fused section. Using thread to match fabrics, machine satin-stitch around each fused shape. Remove fabric stabilizer.

Step 4. Fold each C strip with wrong sides together along length; press.

Step 5. Machine-baste a folded C strip to a D strip as shown in Figure 2; repeat to make four C-D strips.

Figure 2

Step 6. Sew a basted C-D strip to opposite sides of the appliquéd center; press seams toward C-D strips.

Step 7. Sew an E square to each end of the remaining C-D strips; press seams away from E.

Step 8. Sew a C-D-E strip to the top and bottom of the appliquéd center; press seams toward the C-D-E strips.

Step 9. Sew F strips to opposite sides of the appliquéd center; press seams toward F strips.

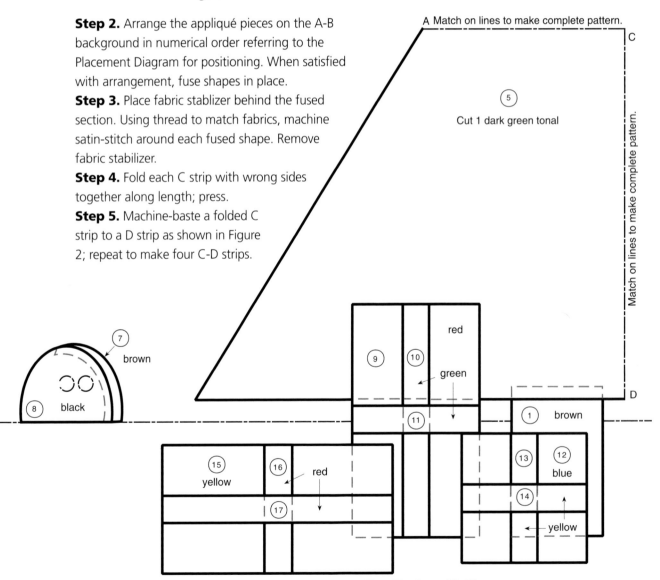

Tree/Package Motif

Step 10. Sew a G square to each end of the remaining F strips; press seams toward F strips.

Step 11. Sew an F-G strip to the top and bottom of the appliquéd center to complete the top.

Step 12. Quilt and bind referring to Completing Your Quilt on page 173.

Step 13. Hand-stitch jingle bells and spangles to quilted top referring to the Placement Diagram and project photo for positioning.

Step 14. Glue wiggly eyes to mousehole using fabric glue to finish. ❖

Christmas Kitty
Placement Diagram
20½" x 20½"

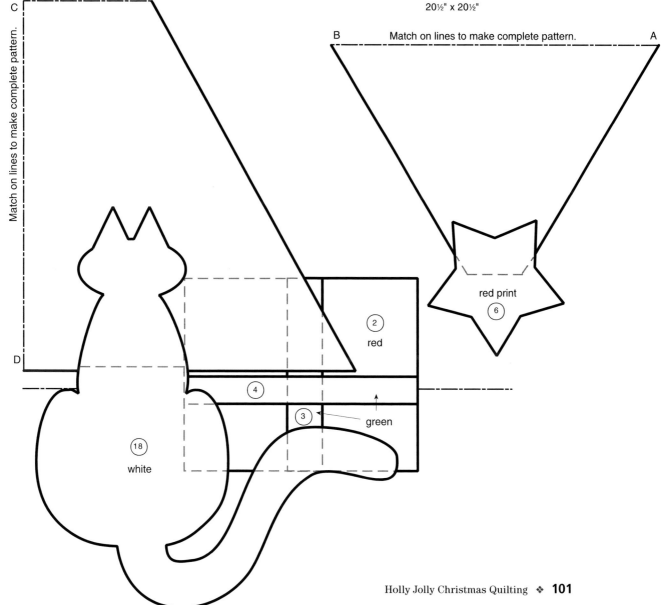

Holiday Stars Pillow

Design by **SANDRA L. HATCH**

Stitch a pillow from fun holiday fabrics to dress up your sofa.

PROJECT SPECIFICATIONS

Skill Level: Beginner
Pillow Size: 16"
   x 16" (without
   ruffle)
Block Size: 16" x 16"
Number of Blocks: 1

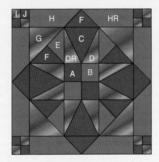

Holiday Stars
16" x 16" Block

MATERIALS

- 1 fat quarter each
  red and green star tonals
- ½ yard holiday print
- ⅝ yard coordinating stripe
- Batting 18" x 18"
- Lining 18" x 18"
- All-purpose thread to match fabrics
- 16" x 16" pillow form
- Basic sewing tools and supplies

CUTTING

Step 1. Prepare templates using pattern pieces given; cut as directed on each piece.
Step 2. Cut two 2½" x 2½" squares each red (A) and green star (B) tonals.
Step 3. Cut one 5¼" x 5¼" square green star tonal (E) and two red tonal (F). Cut each square

in half on both diagonals to make four E and eight F triangles.
Step 4. Cut eight 1½" x 1½" squares each red tonal (J) and holiday print (I).
Step 5. Cut two 4⅞" x 4⅞" squares holiday print; cut each square in half on one diagonal to make four G triangles.
Step 6. Cut two 12" x 16½" rectangles holiday print for pillow back pieces.
Step 7. Cut three 6½" by fabric width strips co-ordinating stripe for ruffle.

COMPLETING THE BLOCK

Step 1. Sew A to B; press seam toward B. Repeat to make two A-B units. Join as shown in Figure 1 to complete the center unit.

Figure 1   **Figure 2**

Step 2. Sew D and DR to C as shown in Figure 2; press seams toward D and DR. Repeat to make four C-D units.
Step 3. Sew E to F to make an E-F unit as shown in Figure 3; press seam toward F. Repeat to make two each E-F and reversed E-F units, again refer-ring to Figure 3.

Figure 3

Reversed

Figure 4

Step 4. Sew G to an E-F unit to complete a corner unit as shown in Figure 4; press seam toward G. Repeat to make two each corner and reversed corner units, again referring to Figure 4.

Step 5. Sew a C-D unit between a corner unit

and a reversed corner unit as shown in Figure 5 to make the top row; press seams toward the corner units. Repeat to make the bottom row.

Step 6. Sew the A-B center unit between two C-D units as shown in Figure 6 to make the center row; press seams toward the center row.

Figure 5

Figure 6

Step 7. Sew the center row between the top and bottom rows to complete the block center referring to Figure 7; press seams toward the center row.

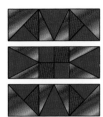

Figure 7

Step 8. Sew H and HR to F to make an F-H unit as shown in Figure 8; press seams toward H and HR. Repeat to make four F-H units.

Figure 8

Step 9. Sew an F-H unit to opposite sides of the pieced center as shown in Figure 9; press seams toward the F-H units.

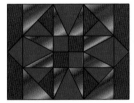

Figure 9

Step 10. Sew J to I; repeat to make eight I-J units. Press seams toward J.

Step 11. Join two I-J units to make an I-J corner unit as shown in Figure 10; press seam in one direction. Repeat to make four I-J corner units.

Figure 10   **Figure 11**

Step 12. Sew an I-J corner unit to each end of each remaining F-H unit to make the side rows as shown in Figure 11; press seams toward the F-H units.

Step 13. Sew the side rows to the remaining

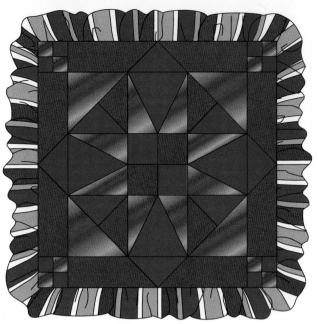

Holiday Stars Pillow
Placement Diagram
16" x 16" (without ruffle)

sides of the pieced center to complete the block; press seams toward the side rows.

COMPLETING THE PILLOW

Step 1. Sandwich the batting square between the completed block and lining square; pin or baste to hold.

Step 2. Quilt as desired by hand or machine; remove pins or basting. Trim edges even to complete the pillow top.

Step 3. Join the ruffle strips with right sides together on the short ends to make a tube; press seams open.

Step 4. Fold the tube in half with wrong sides together to make a double layer; press.

Step 5. Stitch two rows of machine gathering stitches along the raw edges of the layered ruffle as shown in Figure 12.

Figure 12

Step 6. Divide the ruffle into four equal sections; mark with pins.

Step 7. Pull the bottom threads to gather ruffle to fit quilted pillow top, matching one section to each side of the pillow and adjusting gathers to fit; pin in place.

Step 8. Machine-baste gathered ruffle to pillow edges as shown in Figure 13.

Step 9. Fold over one 16½" edge of each 12" x 16½" backing piece ¼" and press. Fold over ½" again; press and stitch to hem.

Step 10. Place backing pieces right sides together with the quilted pillow top/ruffle layers, overlapping backing pieces as needed as shown in Figure 14; stitch all around edges.

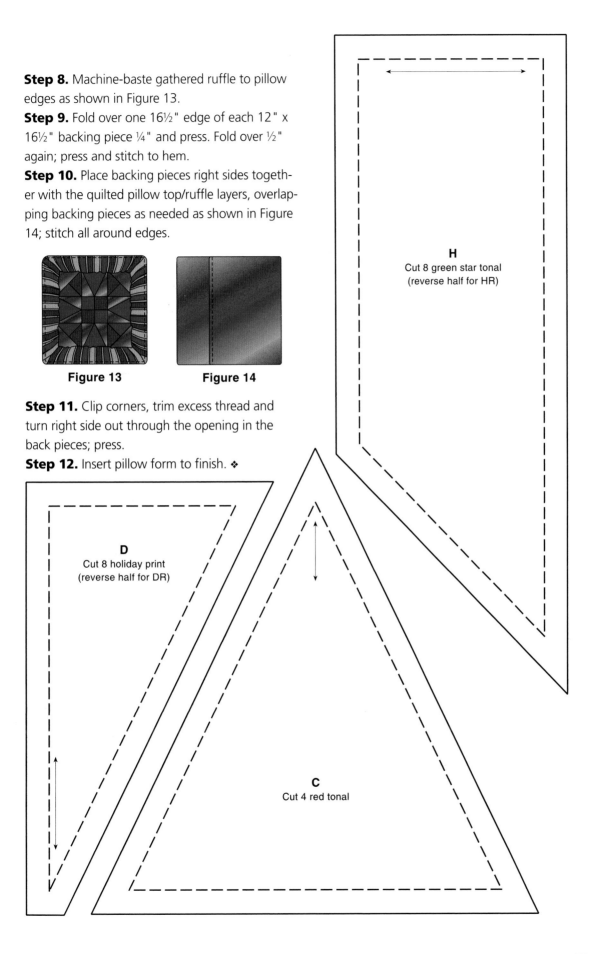

Figure 13   **Figure 14**

Step 11. Clip corners, trim excess thread and turn right side out through the opening in the back pieces; press.

Step 12. Insert pillow form to finish. ❖

H
Cut 8 green star tonal
(reverse half for HR)

D
Cut 8 holiday print
(reverse half for DR)

C
Cut 4 red tonal

Flannel Fun Throw

Design by **CHRIS MALONE**

Fringed shapes take on new looks in this flannel throw.

PROJECT SPECIFICATIONS

Skill Level: Beginner
Quilt Size:
43½" x 43½"
Block Size: 7½" x 7½"
Number of Blocks: 25

MATERIALS

All fabrics are flannel.

- ⅛ yard brown solid
- 1 yard tan speckled
- 1 yard red speckled
- 1¾ yards green speckled
- Backing 50" x 50"
- Batting 50" x 50"
- All-purpose thread to match fabrics
- Quilting thread
- No. 5 tan pearl cotton
- 48 (⅝") red buttons
- 13 (⅞") 2-hole buttons in any color
- No-fray solution
- Basic sewing tools and supplies

CUTTING

Step 1. Cut three 8" by fabric width strips tan speckled; subcut strips into (12) 8" A squares.

Step 2. Cut one 3" by fabric width D strip tan speckled.

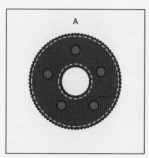

Wreath
7½" x 7½" Block
Make 6

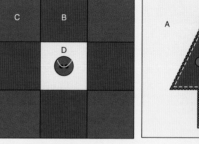

Nine-Patch
7½" x 7½" Block
Make 13

Tree
7½" x 7½" Block
Make 6

Step 3. Cut four 3" by fabric width B strips green speckled.

Step 4. Cut two 3½" x 38" E strips and two 3½" x 44" F strips along the length of the green speckled.

Step 5. Cut four 3" by fabric width C strips red speckled.

Step 6. Cut five 2½" by fabric width strips red speckled for binding.

Step 7. Prepare templates for button cover, wreath, tree and trunk shapes using patterns given; cut as directed on each piece.

COMPLETING THE NINE-PATCH BLOCKS

Step 1. Sew a B strip between two C strips with right sides together along the length to make a B-C strip set; press seams toward C strip. Repeat to make two B-C strip sets.

Step 2. Subcut the B-C strip sets into (26) 3" B-C units as shown in Figure 1.

Figure 1

Figure 2

Figure 3

Step 3. Sew the D strip between two B strips with right sides together along the length to make a B-D strip set; press seams toward B.

Step 4. Subcut the B-D strip set into (13) 3" B-D units as shown in Figure 2.

Step 5. Sew a B-D unit between two B-C units to complete one Nine-Patch block as shown in Figure 3; press seams toward the B-C units. Repeat to make 13 Nine-Patch blocks.

FLANNEL FUN THROW

COMPLETING THE TREE BLOCKS

Step 1. Pin two tree shapes together with right sides up; sew all around ½" from the edges, as shown in Figure 4, using thread to match fabric. Repeat for all tree shapes.

Step 2. Repeat Step 1 with trunk shapes, leaving one short end unstitched as shown in Figure 4.

Figure 4   **Figure 5**

Step 3. Clip every ¼"–⅝" almost to the stitched lines on the tree and trunk shapes except at tree corners as shown in Figure 5.

Step 4. Center one tree and trunk motif on the right side on an A square, tucking the unstitched edge of the trunk piece under the tree piece as shown in Figure 6.

Figure 6   **Figure 7**

Step 5. Sew on the previously stitched lines and from the stitched lines to the corners of trees to stabilize as shown in Figure 7.

Step 6. Sew three ⅝" red buttons to the tree referring to the block drawing and quilt photo for positioning of buttons to complete one Tree block. Repeat to make six blocks.

COMPLETING THE WREATH BLOCKS

Step 1. Pin two wreath shapes together with right sides up; stitch ½" from edges all around with matching thread.

Step 2. Make clips around inside and outside edges to the stitching line ¼"–⅜" apart as shown in Figure 8.

Figure 8

Step 3. Center a wreath on the right side of an A

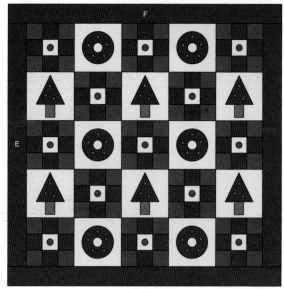

Flannel Fun Throw
Placement Diagram
43½" x 43½"

square; stitch on previously stitched lines.

Step 4. Sew five ⅝" red buttons around the wreath referring to the block drawing and quilt photo for positioning of buttons to complete one Wreath block; repeat to make six blocks.

COMPLETING THE QUILT

Step 1. Join two Wreath blocks with three Nine-Patch blocks to make a wreath row as shown in Figure 9; press seams toward Wreath blocks. Repeat to make three wreath rows.

Figure 9

Step 2. Join two Nine-Patch blocks with three Tree blocks to make a tree row as shown in Figure 10; press seams toward Tree blocks. Repeat to make two tree rows.

Figure 10

Step 3. Join the rows referring to the Placement Diagram for positioning of rows; press seams in one direction.

Step 4. Sew E strips to opposite sides and F strips to the top and bottom of the pieced center; press seams toward E and F strips.

Step 5. Apply no-fray solution to the button-cover circles.

Step 6. Hand-gather around the edge of each circle and place a ⅞" button on the wrong side of the fabric as shown in Figure 11; pull the thread to gather edges together to cover the button. Knot the thread to hold.

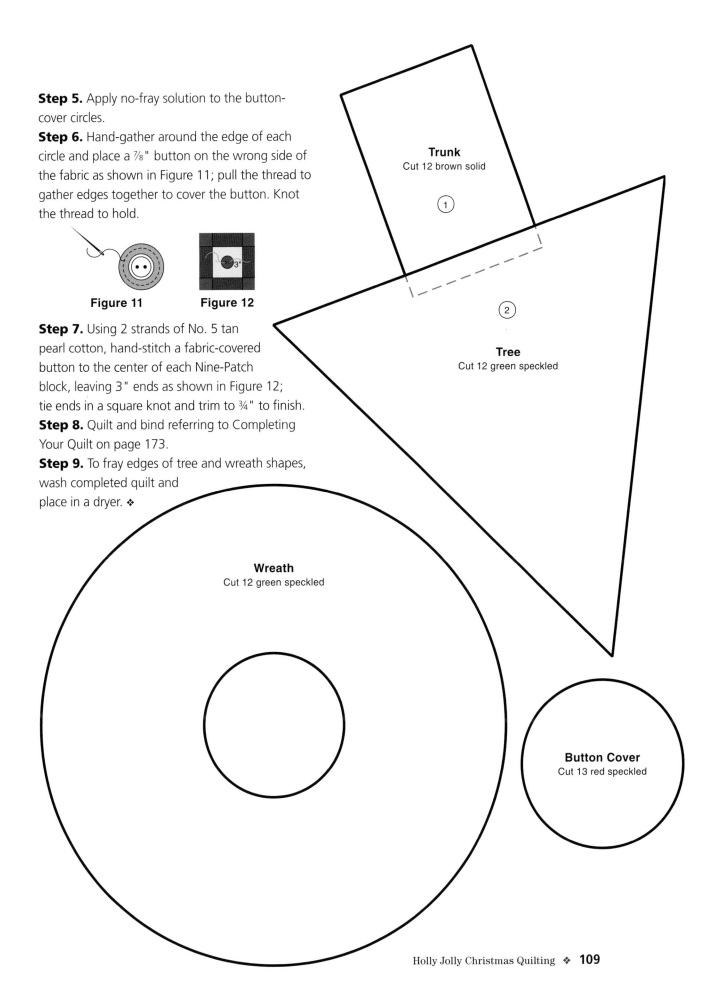

Figure 11

Figure 12

Step 7. Using 2 strands of No. 5 tan pearl cotton, hand-stitch a fabric-covered button to the center of each Nine-Patch block, leaving 3" ends as shown in Figure 12; tie ends in a square knot and trim to ¾" to finish.

Step 8. Quilt and bind referring to Completing Your Quilt on page 173.

Step 9. To fray edges of tree and wreath shapes, wash completed quilt and place in a dryer. ❖

Trunk
Cut 12 brown solid

① 1

② 2

Tree
Cut 12 green speckled

Wreath
Cut 12 green speckled

Button Cover
Cut 13 red speckled

Buttons in My Cabin

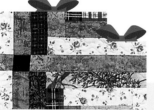

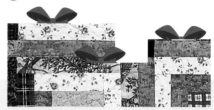

Design by **BETTY ALDERMAN**

Join traditional Log Cabin blocks with button centers to make this pretty throw.

PROJECT SPECIFICATIONS

Skill Level: Beginner
Quilt Size:
  49¾" x 49¾"
Block Size: 10" x 10"
Number of Blocks: 16

MATERIALS

- Light and dark print or plaid scraps for log pieces
- Black print scrap
- ⅛ yard black tonal
- ¼ yard dark red mottled
- ⅜ yard each medium red and medium green mottleds
- ¾ yard dark green print
- Batting 55" x 55"
- Backing 55" x 55"
- Neutral color all-purpose thread
- Clear nylon monofilament
- Red pearl cotton
- 16 (⅝") bone-color buttons
- 7 yards black jumbo rickrack
- Basic sewing tools and supplies

Log Cabin
10" x 10" Block

CUTTING

Step 1. Cut two 3" by fabric width strips dark red mottled; subcut strips into (16) 3" A squares.

Step 2. Cut light-color scraps into 1¾"-wide strips; subcut strips into 16 pieces each as follows: 3" B, 4¼" C, 5½" F, 6¾" G, 8" J and 9¼" K.

Step 3. Cut dark-color scraps into 1¾"-wide strips; subcut strips into 16 pieces each as follows: 4¼" D, 5½" E, 6¾" H, 8" I, 9¼" L and 10½" M.

Step 4. Cut one 10½" by fabric width strip each medium red (N) and medium green (O) mottleds; subcut strips into (20) 1¾" strips each for N and O.

Step 5. Cut two 1¾" by fabric width strips black tonal; subcut strips into (25) 1¾" P squares.

Step 6. Cut five 2¼" by fabric width strips dark green print. Join strips on short ends to make one long strip; press seams open. Subcut strip into four 46¾" Q strips.

Step 7. Cut five 2¼" by fabric width strips dark green print for binding.

Step 8. Cut four 2¼" x 2¼" R squares black print.

COMPLETING THE BLOCKS

Step 1. Sew B to A; press seam toward B. Repeat for all A and B pieces.

Step 2. Continue adding pieces to the block centers in alphabetical order to complete 16 Log

BUTTONS IN MY CABIN

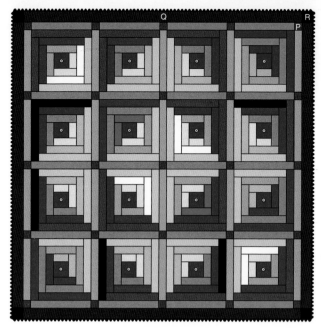

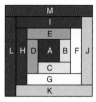

Cabin blocks as shown in Figure 1, pressing seams away from the block center after each addition.

Figure 1

COMPLETING THE QUILT

Step 1. Join four Log Cabin blocks with five N strips to make a block row referring to Figure 2; press seams toward N strips. Repeat to make four block rows.

Figure 2

Step 2. Join four O strips with five P quares to make a sashing row referring to Figure 3; press seams toward O strips. Repeat to make five sashing rows.

Figure 3

Step 3. Join the block rows with the sashing rows to complete the pieced center; press seams toward the sashing rows.

Step 4. Sew a Q strip to opposite sides of the pieced center; press seams toward the Q strips.

Step 5. Sew an R square to each end of each re-maining Q strip; press seams toward the Q strips. Sew the Q-R strips to the remaining sides of the pieced center to complete the pieced top; press seams toward the Q-R strips.

Step 6. Layer, quilt and prepare binding referring to the General Instructions on page 173. *Note: Use clear nylon monofilament for quilting.*

Step 7. Cut four 52" lengths black jumbo rick-rack; pin one length to each side of the pieced top referring to Figure 4; machine-baste in place to hold.

Figure 4

Buttons in My Cabin
Placement Diagram
49¾" x 49¾"

Step 8. Cut the binding strip into four 52" lengths.

Step 9. Pin raw edges of binding even with two opposite raw edges of the quilt top, on top of the jumbo rickrack as shown in Figure 5; stitch. Trim ends even as shown in Figure 6.

Figure 5   **Figure 6**

Step 10. Turn the binding to the back side and hand-stitch in place with rickrack extending at the edges of the quilt top as shown in the close-up photo.

Step 11. Center and stitch the remaining two binding strips on the remaining sides of the quilt-ed top; trim ends to ½". Turn ends in as shown in Figure 7.

Figure 7

Step 12. Turn the binding to the back side and hand-stitch in place as in Step 10.

Step 13. Sew a ⅝" bone-color button to the A center of each block using red pearl cotton to finish. ❖

Holly Wreath

Design by **SUE HARVEY**

Simple fused holly leaves are curled to add dimension to the centerpiece of this quilt.

PROJECT SPECIFICATIONS

Skill Level: Intermediate
Quilt Size: 40⅜" x 40⅜"
Block Size: 4¼" x 6⅜"
Number of Blocks: 8

MATERIALS

- ⅛ yard red dot
- ¼ yard each two medium green dots
- ½ yard red holly print
- ½ yard gold dot
- ½ yard light green dot
- ½ yard dark green print
- ¾ yard gold holly print
- 1¼ yards dark green dot
- Backing 46" x 46"
- Batting 46" x 46"
- Neutral color, red and green all-purpose thread
- Quilting thread

Nine-Patch X
4¼" x 6⅜" Block

- 1¼ yards heavyweight fusible web
- 8 (½") red buttons
- Wooden pencil
- Basic tools and supplies

CUTTING

Step 1. Cut two 6⅞" by fabric width strips red holly print; subcut strips into eight 6⅞" A squares and four 3⅜" x 3⅜" I squares. Cut each I square on both diagonals to make 16 I triangles.

Step 2. Cut four 2⅝" by fabric width strips gold dot; subcut strips into (60) 2⅝" B squares.

Step 3. Cut one 2" by fabric width E strip gold dot; subcut strip into two 21"-long strips. Discard one strip.

Step 4. Cut one 3" by fabric width strip gold dot; subcut strip into (10) 3" squares. Cut each square in half on one diagonal to make 20 J triangles.

Step 5. Cut one 2⅝" by fabric width strip gold holly print; subcut strip into (12) 2⅝" C squares.

Step 6. Cut one 2" by fabric width G strip gold holly print; subcut strip into two 21"-long strips. Discard one strip.

Step 7. Cut one 15⅜" x 15⅜" N square and eight 3" x 3" H squares gold holly print; cut each H square in half on one diagonal to make 16 H triangles.

Step 8. Cut two 2" by fabric width D strips light green dot; subcut strips into four 21"-long strips.

Step 9. Cut one 8" x 21" strip light green dot for holly leaves.

Step 10. Cut one 2" by fabric width F strip red dot; subcut strip into two 21"-long strips. Discard one strip.

Step 11. Cut three 2⅝" by fabric width strips dark green print; subcut strips into (12) 6⅞" K strips and eight 4¾" L strips.

Step 12. Cut two 3" x 3" squares dark green print; cut each square in half on one diagonal to make four M triangles.

Step 13. Cut two strips each 4¾" x 32⅜" for O and 4¾" x 40⅞" for P from dark green dot.

Step 14. Cut five 2¼" by fabric width strips dark green dot for binding.

Step 15. Cut one 8" x 21" strip dark green dot for holly leaves.

Step 16. Cut one 8" x 21" strip from each medium green dot for holly leaves.

Step 17. Cut two 8" x 21" strips heavyweight fusible web.

PIECING THE A-B-C UNITS
Step 1. Mark a diagonal line from corner to corner on the wrong side of each B and C square.

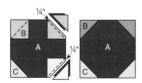

Figure 1   **Figure 2**

Step 2. Place a B square on two adjacent corners and a C square on the remaining two corners of an A square as shown in Figure 1; stitch on the

marked lines, trim seam allowances to ¼" and press B and C to the right side to complete one A-B-C unit, again referring to Figure 1. Repeat to make four A-B-C units.

Step 3. Repeat Step 2 with three B squares and one C square to complete an A-B-C corner unit as shown in Figure 2; repeat to make four A-B-C corner units.

PIECING THE BLOCKS
Step 1. Sew a D strip to an E strip with right sides together along length to complete a strip set; press seam toward D.

Step 2. Cut the strip set into eight 2" D-E units as shown in Figure 3.

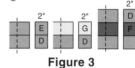

Figure 3

Step 3. Repeat Steps 1 and 2 with D and G strips to make eight 2" D-G units, again referring to Figure 3.

Step 4. Sew an F strip between two D strips to make a strip set; press seams toward D. Cut the strip set into eight 2" D-F units, again referring to Figure 3.

Step 5. Sew an I triangle to the D end of each D-E and D-G unit to complete D-E-I and D-G-I units as shown in Figure 4.

Figure 4   **Figure 5**   **Figure 6**

Step 6. To piece one Nine-Patch X block, join one of each pieced unit as shown in Figure 5; press seams away from the D-F unit.

Step 7. Sew a J triangle to the two D-E edges of the pieced unit and an H triangle to the two D-G edges to complete one block as shown in Figure 6; press seams toward J and H. Repeat to make eight blocks.

PIECING THE BORDER UNITS

Step 1. Place a B square right sides together on each end of K as shown in Figure 7; stitch, trim and press B to the right side as for the A-B-C units to complete a B-K unit. Repeat to make 12 B-K units.

Figure 7

Step 2. Place B right sides together on one end of L as shown in Figure 8; stitch, trim and press B to the right side. Repeat on the remaining end of L to complete one B-L unit, again referring to Figure 8. Repeat to make eight B-L units.

Figure 8

Step 3. Sew J to M along the diagonal to make a J-M unit; press seam toward M. Repeat to make four J-M units.

COMPLETING THE QUILT

Step 1. Sew an A-B-C unit between two Nine-Patch X blocks as shown in Figure 9; press seams toward the A-B-C units. Repeat to make four pieced strips.

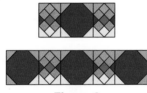

Figure 9

Step 2. Sew a pieced strip to two opposite sides of N referring to the Placement Diagram for positioning; press seams toward N.

Step 3. Sew an A-B-C corner unit to each end of the remaining pieced strips, again referring to Figure 9; press seams toward the A-B-C corner units.

Step 4. Sew a pieced strip to the remaining sides of N, again referring to the Placement Diagram for positioning; press seams toward N.

Step 5. Join three B-K units with two B-L units to make a strip as shown in Figure 10; press seams toward the B-L units. Repeat to make four strips.

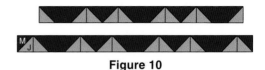

Figure 10

Step 6. Sew a strip to two opposite sides of the pieced center referring to the Placement Diagram for positioning; press seams toward strips.

Step 7. Sew a J-M unit to each end of the remaining strips, again referring to Figure 10; press seams away from J-M.

Step 8. Sew a strip to the remaining sides of the pieced center, again referring to the Placement Diagram for positioning; press seams toward strips.

Step 9. Sew O to opposite sides and P to the remaining sides of the pieced center to complete the pieced top; press seams toward O and P.

Step 10. Layer, quilt and bind referring to Completing Your Quilt on page 173.

ADDING THE WREATH

Step 1. Wash and dry the 8" x 21" holly leaf fabric strips; do not use fabric softener or dryer sheets.

Step 2. Apply a fusible web strip to the wrong side of the dark green dot strip; remove paper backing.

Step 3. Fuse one medium green dot strip to the dark green dot strip.

Step 4. Repeat Steps 2 and 3 with the light green dot and remaining medium green dot strips.

Step 5. Prepare a template for the holly leaf shape.

Step 6. Trace 12 leaves on each fused strip; cut out.

Step 7. Reheat a dark/medium leaf shape with a hot, dry iron. Immediately fold the hot leaf shape over the wooden pencil with the dark side toward the pencil as shown in Figure 11; hold until cool. Repeat to make eight dark curled leaves.

Step 8. Repeat Step 7 to make

Figure 11

eight light curled leaves and four curled leaves of each medium green.

Step 9. Arrange the eight dark leaves in a circle on the center N square of the quilt, placing a leaf at the center of each side and one on each diagonal as shown in Figure 12; pin in place.

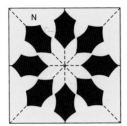

Figure 12

Step 10. Using green all-purpose thread, straight-stitch a line through the center of each leaf referring to the pattern for placement.

Step 11. Place a medium green leaf between each dark green leaf as shown in Figure 13; pin and stitch in place.

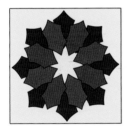

Figure 13

Step 12. Arrange the light green leaves over the medium green leaves referring to the Placement Diagram and Figure 14 for positioning; pin and stitch in place.

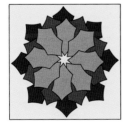

Figure 14

Step 13. Hand-stitch a red button on the inside point of each light green leaf to finish referring to the Placement Diagram for positioning. ❖

Holly Wreath
Placement Diagram
40⅜" x 40⅜"

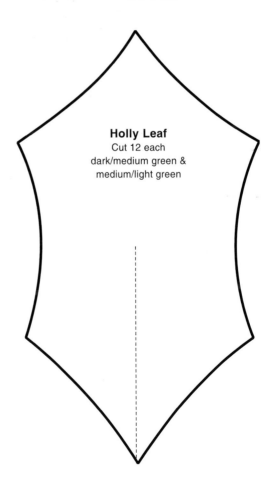

Holly Leaf
Cut 12 each
dark/medium green &
medium/light green

Gingerbread Patchwork

Design by **JUDITH SANDSTROM**

Use an assortment of narrow, fabric width strips to create this patchwork throw.

PROJECT NOTE
Whether you purchase specific fabrics or use strips cut from your fabric collection, select half Christmas prints and half red and green tonals, including small checks or plaids.

PROJECT SPECIFICATIONS
Skill Level: Beginner
Quilt Size: 36" x 44"

MATERIALS
- ⅛ yard each 19 Christmas prints
- ¼ yard brown tonal
- ⅜ yard green tonal
- ½ yard cream tonal
- Backing 42" x 50"
- Batting 42" x 50"
- All-purpose thread to match fabrics
- Quilting thread
- ⅝ yard fusible web
- ⅝ yard fabric stabilizer
- Assorted beads
- Basic sewing tools and supplies

CUTTING
Step 1. Cut two 6½" by fabric width strips cream tonal; subcut strips into (12) 4½" A rectangles.
Step 2. Cut one 2½" by fabric width strip from each of the 19 Christmas prints.
Step 3. Trace 12 gingerbread-man shapes onto the paper side of the fusible web using pattern given.
Step 4. Iron the fusible web to the wrong side of the brown tonal; cut out shapes along traced lines. Remove paper backing.
Step 5. Cut (12) 4" x 6" rectangles fabric stabilizer.
Step 6. Cut four 2¼" by fabric width binding strips green tonal.

COMPLETING THE QUILT
Step 1. Center a gingerbread-man motif on each A rectangle; fuse in place.
Step 2. Center a piece of fabric stabilizer on the wrong side of each fused A rectangle; pin to hold in place.
Step 3. Using thread to match brown tonal and a medium-width zigzag stitch, sew around each fused shape.

Gingerbread Patchwork
Placement Diagram
36" x 44"

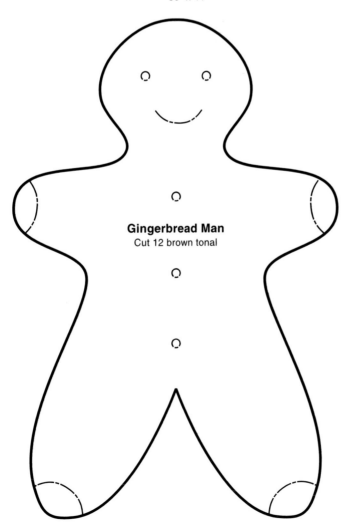

Gingerbread Man
Cut 12 brown tonal

Step 4. When all stitching is complete, remove fabric stabilizer.

Step 5. Organize the 2½"-wide strips into five groups of two strips each and three groups of three strips each. ***Note:*** *Use any larger Christmas prints in the two-strip groups because they will be cut into larger pieces.*

Step 6. Stitch the strips into two-strip or three-strip strip sets with right sides together along the length; press seams open.

Step 7. Subcut each two-strip set into six 6½" B units as shown in Figure 1.

B unit
6½"

Figure 1

Step 8. Subcut each three-strip set into (16) 2½" C units as shown in Figure 2.

C unit
2½"

Figure 2

Step 9. Arrange six appliquéd A rectangles with B and C units into three vertical rows as shown in Figure 3; join to make vertical rows. Press seams open.

Step 10. Join the vertical rows to complete half of the quilt top; press seams open. Repeat to make the second half of the top in the same manner. Join the two halves to complete the pieced top.

Step 11. Complete the quilt referring to Completing Your Quilt on page 173.

Step 12. Hand-stitch beads to each appliquéd gingerbread man referring to pattern for positioning to finish. ❖

Figure 3

Christmas Snow Globes

Design by **SUE HARVEY**

Easy-to-piece snow globes show off
fussy-cut preprinted squares.

PROJECT SPECIFICATIONS

Skill Level: Beginner
Quilt Size:
$42^{5/8}$" x $56^{3/8}$"
Block Size:
11" x $9^{5/8}$"
Number of Blocks: 6

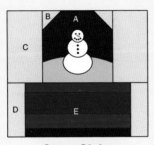

Snow Globe
11" x $9^{5/8}$" Block

MATERIALS

- Six 6" x 6" motifs for A
- $1/3$ yard lengthwise stripe
- $2/3$ yard tan speckled
- $3/4$ yard black speckled
- 1 yard red tonal
- $1^{3/4}$ yards reindeer print
- Batting 49" x 63"
- Backing 49" x 63"
- Neutral color all-purpose thread
- Quilting thread
- Basic sewing tools and supplies

CUTTING

Step 1. Cut one 2" by fabric width strip tan speckled; subcut strip into (12) 2" B squares.

Step 2. Cut one 6" by fabric width strip tan speckled; subcut strip into (12) $3^{1/4}$" C rectangles.

Step 3. Cut one $4^{5/8}$" by fabric width strip tan speckled; subcut strip into (12) $1^{7/8}$" D rectangles.

Step 4. Cut three $1^{7/8}$" by fabric width F strips tan speckled.

Step 5. Cut six $4^{5/8}$" x $8^{3/4}$" E rectangles along the length of the stripe.

Step 6. Cut four $1^{7/8}$" by fabric width G strips black speckled.

Step 7. Cut five $2^{1/4}$" by fabric width strips black speckled for binding.

Step 8. Cut two $1^{7/8}$" by fabric width strips red tonal; subcut strips into eight $1^{7/8}$" H squares, four $3^{1/4}$" I rectangles and eight $4^{5/8}$" J rectangles.

Step 9. Cut four $1^{7/8}$" by fabric width strips red tonal; subcut strips into four $23^{7/8}$" K strips and three $10^{1/8}$" L strips.

Step 10. Cut two strips red tonal each $1^{7/8}$" x $37^{5/8}$" (M), $1^{7/8}$" x $26^{5/8}$" (N) and $1^{7/8}$" x $32^{1/8}$" (P).

Step 11. Cut two $1^{7/8}$" by fabric width strips red tonal; prepare two $43^{1/8}$" O strips using ends of strips cut into Step 10. ***Note:*** *The fabric used in the sample has a $43^{1/2}$" usable width so no piecing was needed for the O strips.*

Step 12. Cut two 6" x $43^{1/8}$" R strips across the width and two 6" x $45^{7/8}$" Q strips along the

length of the reindeer print. **Note:** *The fabric used in the sample has a 43½" usable width. If your fabric does not, cut the Q strips along the length first, and then cut three strips across the remaining width to join and cut the 43⅛" R strips.*

COMPLETING THE BLOCKS

Step 1. Mark a diagonal line from corner to corner on the wrong side of each B square.

Step 2. Place a B square right sides together on adjacent top corners of each A square as shown in Figure 1; stitch on the marked line, trim seam allowance to ¼" and press B to the right side to complete six A-B units, again referring to Figure 1.

Figure 1   **Figure 2**

Step 3. Sew C to opposite sides of each A-B unit as shown in Figure 2; press seams toward C.

Step 4. Sew D to each end of the E rectangles as shown in Figure 3; press seams toward D.

Figure 3

Step 5. Join the A-B-C and D-E units to complete six Snow Globe blocks referring to the block drawing for positioning of units; press seams toward D-E.

COMPLETING THE PIECED SASHING & BORDER STRIPS

Step 1. Join four G strips with three F strips with right sides together along the length to make a strip set as shown in Figure 4; press seams toward G.

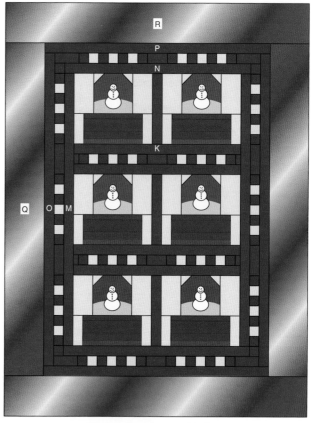

Christmas Snow Globes
Placement Diagram
42⅝" x 56⅜"

Step 2. Subcut the strip set into (14) 1⅞" F-G units, again referring to Figure 4.

Step 3. Join two F-G units with an I rectangle and two H squares as shown in Figure 5; press seams toward H and I. Trim the strip to 23⅞" long with I centered to complete a sashing strip, again referring to Figure 5. Repeat to make two sashing strips.

Figure 5

Step 4. Join two F-G units with an I rectangle and two J rectangles as shown in Figure 6; press seams toward I and J to complete a top border strip. Repeat for a bottom border strip.

Figure 4

Figure 6

Figure 7

Step 5. Join three F-G units with two H squares and two J rectangles as shown in Figure 7; press seams toward H and J to complete a side border strip. Repeat to make a second side border strip.

COMPLETING THE QUILT

Step 1. Join two blocks with L to make a block row as shown in Figure 8; press seams toward L. Repeat to make three block rows.

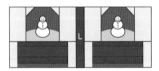

Figure 8

Step 2. Sew a K strip to each long side of the sashing strips; press seams toward K.

Step 3. Join the block rows with the K/sashing strips to complete the pieced center referring to the Placement Diagram for positioning of strips; press seams toward the K/sashing strips.

Step 4. Sew the M strips to opposite long sides and N strips to the top and bottom of the pieced center; press seams toward M and N strips.

Step 5. Sew a pieced side border strip to opposite long sides and the pieced top and bottom border strips to the top and bottom of the pieced center; press seams toward M and N strips.

Step 6. Sew O and P strips and Q and R strips to opposite long sides and then the top and bottom of the pieced center to complete the top; press seams toward strips after each addition.

Step 7. Quilt and bind referring to Completing Your Quilt on page 173. ❖

Holly Jolly Snowmen

Design by **JULIE WEAVER**

Pieced trees and appliquéd snowmen make the perfect holiday wall quilt.

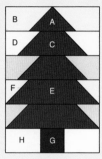

Tree
8" x 12" Block
Make 4

Snowman
8" x 12" Block
Make 5

PROJECT SPECIFICATIONS

Skill Level: Beginner
Quilt Size: 40" x 52"
Block Size: 8" x 12"
Number of Blocks: 9

MATERIALS

Fabrics used have a 42½" usable width.
- Scraps red, gold, blue, orange, brown and white
- ⅛ yard brown print
- ⅝ yard green print
- 1⅛ yards red print
- 1⅜ yards total assorted cream/tan tonals
- Backing 46" x 58"
- Batting 46" x 58"
- All-purpose thread to match fabrics and black

- Quilting thread
- Black embroidery floss
- ¾ yard fusible web
- 13 small star buttons (optional)
- 44 white snowflake buttons (optional)
- Black fine-point permanent fabric pen
- Basic sewing tools and supplies

CUTTING

Step 1. Cut the following 2½"-wide pieces from assorted cream/tan tonals: eight 4½" B rectangles, (16) 3½" D rectangles, (16) 2½" F squares and eight 3½" H rectangles.

Step 2. Cut the following 1½"-wide pieces from assorted cream/tan tonals: (10) 4½" J, (20) 8½" K, (10) 6½" L and (10) 10½" M.

Step 3. Cut five 4½" x 6½" I rectangles assorted cream/tan tonals.

Step 4. Cut the following 1½"-wide pieces from assorted cream/tan tonals: 12 each 8½" O and 12½" N strips, and (16) 1½" P squares.

Step 5. Cut four 2½" by fabric width strips green print; subcut strips into four 4½" A, and eight each 6½" C and 8½" E rectangles.

Step 6. Cut four 1½" by fabric width strips green print; subcut strips into two 40½" Q strips and two 30½" R strips.

Step 7. Cut four 2½" x 2½" G squares brown print.

Step 8. Cut four 5½" by fabric width strips red print; subcut strips into two 42½" S strips and two 40½" T strips.

Step 9. Cut five 2¼" by fabric width strips red print for binding.

Step 10. Trace appliqué shapes onto the paper side of the fusible web referring to pattern for number to cut; cut out shapes, leaving a margin around each one. ***Note:*** *The shapes are given in reverse for fusible appliqué. The Corner Snowman Motif will make the two left-facing snowmen. Reverse the patterns to trace the shapes for the two right-facing snowmen.*

Step 11. Fuse shapes to the wrong side of assorted scraps as directed on patterns for color and number to cut; cut out shapes on traced lines. Remove paper backing.

Step 12. Draw eyes and X marks on snowmen faces using black fine-point permanent fabric pen.

COMPLETING THE TREE BLOCKS

Step 1. Place a B rectangle right sides together on one end of A as shown in Figure 1; mark a line from the top corner of B to where it intersects with A, again referring to Figure 1.

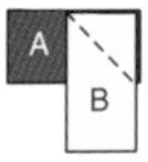

Figure 1

Step 2. Stitch on the marked line; trim excess seam to ¼" and press B to the right side referring to Figure 2.

Figure 2

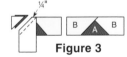

Figure 3

Step 3. Repeat with a second B on the opposite end of A to complete an A-B unit as shown in Figure 3; repeat to make four A-B units.

Step 4. Repeat Steps 1–3 to make eight each C-D and E-F units as shown in Figure 4.

Step 5. Sew G between two H rectangles to make a G-H unit; press seams toward G. Repeat to make four G-H units.

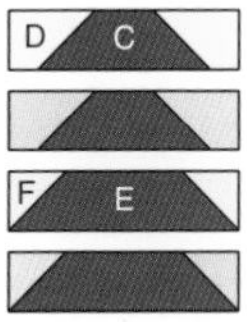

Figure 4 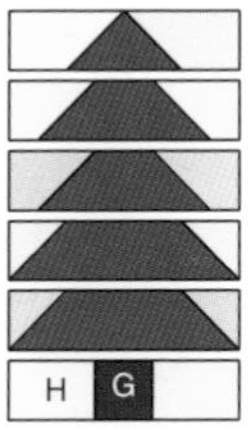   **Figure 5**

Step 6. To complete one Tree block, arrange the pieced units as shown in Figure 5. Join the pieced units and press seams in one direction to complete one block; repeat to make four Tree blocks.

COMPLETING THE SNOWMAN BLOCKS

Step 1. Sew J to opposite short sides of I; press seams toward J.

Step 2. Sew K strips to opposite long sides of the J-I unit; press seams toward K.

Step 3. Continue adding pieces to the short sides and then long sides to complete the block background referring to Figure 6, pressing seams toward the most recently added strips after each addition. Repeat to make five block backgrounds.

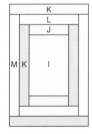

Figure 6

Step 4. Center and arrange a snowman motif on each block background with pieces in numerical order and overlapping as necessary. When satisfied with placement, fuse shapes in place.

Step 5. Using black thread, buttonhole-stitch around each fused shape.

Step 6. If desired, sew three small star buttons to the front of each Corner Snowman and one star button to scarf of Center Snowman as shown on patterns.

COMPLETING THE QUILT

Step 1. Join one Tree block, two Corner Snowman blocks and four N strips to make a row as shown in Figure 7; press seams toward N strips. Repeat to make two rows.

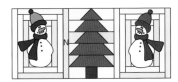

Figure 7

Step 2. Join one Center Snowman block, two Tree blocks and four N strips to make the center row referring to Figure 8; press seams toward N strips.

Figure 8

Step 3. Join three O strips with four P squares to make a sashing row as shown in Figure 9; press seams toward O strips. Repeat to make four sashing rows.

Figure 9

Step 4. Join the block rows with the sashing rows referring to the Placement Diagram for positioning; press seams toward sashing strips.

Step 5. Sew Q strips to opposite long sides and R strips to the top and bottom of the pieced center; press seams toward Q and R strips.

Step 6. Sew S strips to opposite long sides and T strips to the top and bottom of the pieced center; press seams toward S and T strips to complete the pieced top.

Step 7. Quilt and bind referring to Completing Your Quilt on page 173.

Step 8. Hand-stitch snowflake buttons on tree shapes, if desired. ❖

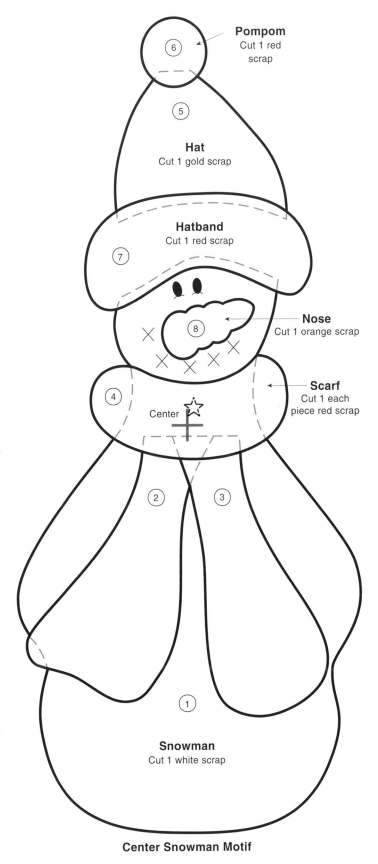

Pompom
Cut 1 red scrap

Hat
Cut 1 gold scrap

Hatband
Cut 1 red scrap

Nose
Cut 1 orange scrap

Scarf
Cut 1 each piece red scrap

Center

Snowman
Cut 1 white scrap

Center Snowman Motif

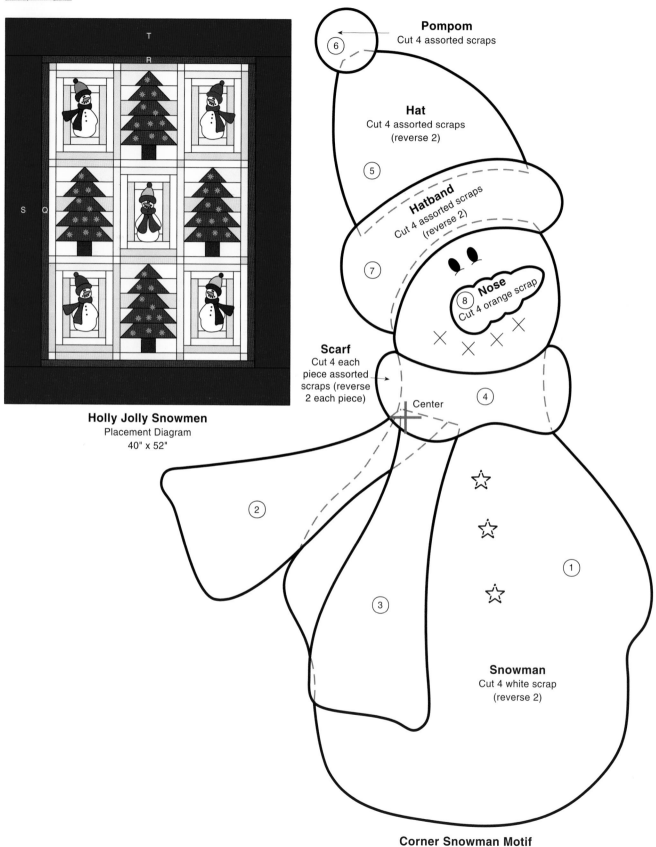

Holly Jolly Snowmen
Placement Diagram
40" x 52"

Pompom
Cut 4 assorted scraps

6

Hat
Cut 4 assorted scraps
(reverse 2)

5

Hatband
Cut 4 assorted scraps
(reverse 2)

7

8 **Nose**
Cut 4 orange scrap

Scarf
Cut 4 each
piece assorted
scraps (reverse
2 each piece)

Center

4

2

3

1

Snowman
Cut 4 white scrap
(reverse 2)

Corner Snowman Motif

Christmas Rose Wreath

Design by **WILLOW ANN SIRCH**

Stitch a holiday wreath design using appliquéd rose motifs to create this festive pillow.

PROJECT SPECIFICATIONS
Skill Level: Intermediate
Pillow Size: 20" x 20"

MATERIALS
- Scraps assorted red, red/gold and green fabrics
- Scrap gold cotton lamé
- 1⅛ yards white-with-gold stars
- All-purpose thread to match fabrics
- Quilting thread
- 20" x 20" pillow form
- 2 (1" x 4") strips hook-and-loop tape
- Water-erasable marker
- Template material
- Basic sewing tools and supplies

CUTTING
Step 1. Using the rose pattern given, prepare a complete rose motif placement template by tracing only the outside lines of the rose pattern.

Step 2. Prepare individual templates for each leaf and B–E rose petals and center using patterns given.

Step 3. Trace rose petals and center, and leaf patterns onto the right side of fabrics as directed on patterns for color and number to cut.

Step 4. Cut out shapes, adding a ⅛"–¼" seam allowance around each shape when cutting.

Step 5. Cut one 20½" x 20½" A square white-with-gold stars.

Step 6. Cut two 12" x 20½" B rectangles white-with-gold stars.

COMPLETING THE PILLOW
Step 1. Fold the A square horizontally, vertically and diagonally and press to mark centers referring to Figure 1.

Figure 1

Step 2. Using the template for the complete rose motif and the water-erasable marker, trace a rose motif 3" from the center on each creased line referring to Figure 2.

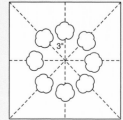

Figure 2

Step 3. Turn under the edges of each leaf shape; baste to hold in place.

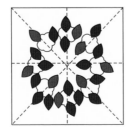

Figure 3

Step 4. Arrange the leaf shapes around the traced rose motifs on A referring to Figure 3; hand-stitch in place. **Note:** *Wherever the leaf shape overlaps the rose motif outlines, the seam allowance on the leaf does not have to be turned under.*

Step 5. Referring to Figure 4 and beginning with B1 petal, arrange and pin pieces in alphabetical/ numerical order to layer one rose motif. Turn under edges of shapes to traced line and hand-stitch in place inside the traced motif. **Note:** *Do not turn under edges where B1 will be covered by other pieces.*

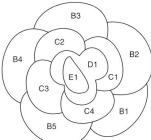

Figure 4

Step 6. Continue turning under edges and hand-stitching pieces inside the traced motif in alphabetical/numerical order to complete one rose motif referring to Figure 5.

Figure 5

Step 7. Repeat Steps 5 and 6 to complete eight rose motifs to complete the pillow top.

Step 8. Turn under ¼" on one 20½" edge of each B rectangle; turn under 1" again and top-stitch to hem.

Step 9. Place the hook pieces of the hook-and-loop tape strips evenly spaced on the wrong side of the hemmed edge of one B rectangle; stitch in place.

Step 10. Place the loop pieces on the right side of the hemmed edge of the remaining B rectangle to align with the hook pieces; stitch in place.

Step 11. Place the backing pieces right sides up with hemmed edges overlapped and hook-and-loop strips attached.

Step 12. Place the appliquéd top right sides together with the backing piece; stitch all around. Clip corners; turn right side out through the back opening and press.

Step 13. Insert the pillow form inside pillow through the back opening to finish. ❖

Christmas Rose Wreath
Placement Diagram
20" x 20"

Leaf
Cut 24 green scraps

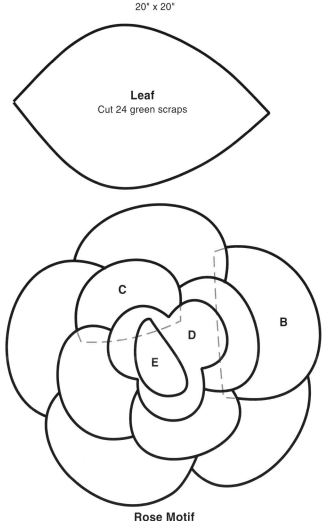

Rose Motif
Cut 40 red B outer petals
Cut 32 red C inner petals
Cut 8 red D 3-petal clusters
Cut 8 gold lamé E centers

Christmas Stars Bed Topper

Design by **SANDRA L. HATCH**

Keep your feet warm while decorating your bed with this holiday bed topper.

PROJECT SPECIFICATIONS

Skill Level: Beginner

Quilt Size:
  71½" x 44½"

Block Size: 12" x 12"

Number of Blocks: 8

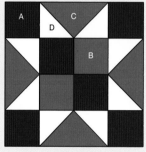

Four-Patch Star
12" x 12" Block

MATERIALS

- ½ yard red tonal
- ⅝ yard snowflake stripe
- ¾ yard white tonal
- ⅞ yard red print
- 1⅜ yards green tonal
- 1¾ yards coordinating stripe
- Backing 78" x 51"
- Batting 78" x 51"
- All-purpose thread to match fabrics
- Quilting thread
- Basic sewing tools and supplies

CUTTING

Step 1. Cut five 3½" by fabric width strips green tonal; subcut three strips into (32) 3½" A squares. Set aside remaining strips for A-B units.

Step 2. Cut one 2" by fabric width strip green tonal; subcut strip into (15) 2" F squares.

Step 3. Cut one 6½" by fabric width strip green tonal; subcut strip into four 6½" L squares.

Step 4. Cut six 2¼" by fabric width strips green tonal for binding.

Step 5. Cut two 3½" by fabric width B strips red print.

Step 6. Cut three 6½" by fabric width strips red print; subcut strips into (32) 3½" C rectangles.

Step 7. Cut six 3½" by fabric width strips white tonal; subcut strips into (64) 3½" D squares. Mark a diagonal line from corner to corner on the wrong side of each square. Trim the remainder of the strip to 2½"; subcut into four 2½" I squares.

Step 8. Cut eight 2" by fabric width strips snowflake stripe; subcut strips into (22) 12½" E strips.

Step 9. Cut three 2½" by fabric width strips red tonal. Join strips on short ends to make one long strip; press seams open. Subcut strip into two 56" G strips.

Step 10. Cut two 2½" x 29" H strips red tonal.

Step 11. Cut two 6½" x 33" K strips and two 6½" x 60" J strips along the length of the coordinating stripe. ***Note:*** *Select a section of the stripe and cut identical sections along the length of the fabric.*

CHRISTMAS STARS BED TOPPER

COMPLETING THE BLOCKS

Step 1. Sew an A strip to a B strip with right sides together along the length; press seams toward B strips. Repeat to make two A-B strip sets.

Step 2. Subcut the A-B strip sets into (16) 3½" A-B units as shown in Figure 1.

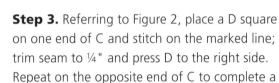

Figure 1   **Figure 2**

Step 3. Referring to Figure 2, place a D square on one end of C and stitch on the marked line; trim seam to ¼" and press D to the right side. Repeat on the opposite end of C to complete a C-D unit. Repeat to make 32 C-D units.

Figure 3   **Figure 4**   **Figure 5**

Step 4. To complete one Four-Patch Star block, join two A-B units to complete the A-B center unit as shown in Figure 3; press seam in one direction.

Step 5. Sew a C-D unit to opposite sides of the A-B center unit to complete the center row as shown in Figure 4; press seams toward the A-B center unit.

Step 6. Sew an A square to each end of two C-D units to complete the top and bottom rows as shown in Figure 5; press seams toward A.

Step 7. Sew the pieced rows to the completed center row referring to Figure 6 to complete one block; press seams toward the center row. Repeat to make eight blocks.

Figure 6

COMPLETING THE QUILT

Step 1. Join four blocks with five E strips to make

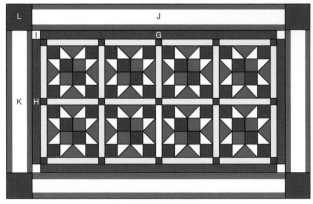

Christmas Stars Bed Topper
Placement Diagram
71½" x 44½"

a block row referring to Figure 7; press seams toward E strips. Repeat to make two block rows.

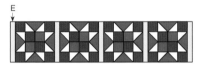

Figure 7

Step 2. Join four E strips with five F squares to make a sashing row referring to Figure 8; press seams toward E strips. Repeat to make three sashing rows.

Figure 8

Step 3. Join the block rows with the sashing rows to complete the pieced center referring to the Placement Diagram for positioning of rows; press seams toward sashing rows.

Step 4. Sew a G strip to opposite long sides of the pieced center; press seams toward G strips.

Step 5. Sew an I square to each end of each H strip; press seams toward H. Sew an H-I strip to opposite short sides of the pieced center; press seams toward the H-I strips.

Step 6. Sew a J strip to opposite long sides of the pieced center; press seams toward J strips.

Step 7. Sew an L square to each end of each K strip; press seams toward L. Sew an L-K strip to opposite short ends of the pieced center to complete the pieced top; press seams toward the L-K strips.

Step 8. Quilt and bind referring to Completing Your Quilt on page 173. ❖

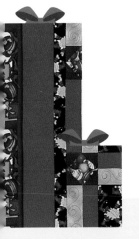

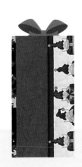

Christmas Fun

Design by **SANDRA L. HATCH**

Select a novelty print to frame in this festive quilt.

PROJECT SPECIFICATIONS
Skill Level: Beginner
Quilt Size: 79" x 92"

MATERIALS
- ⅝ yard ornament print
- ¾ yard green mottled
- 1⅜ yards gold mottled
- 2¼ yards red tonal
- 2½ yards coordinating stripe
- 2½ yards black novelty print
- Backing 85" x 98"
- Batting 85" x 98"
- All-purpose thread to match fabrics
- Quilting thread
- Basic sewing tools and supplies

CUTTING
Step 1. Cut five 9½" by fabric width strips black novelty print; subcut strips into (20) 9½" A squares.

Step 2. Cut seven 2" by fabric width strips black novelty print. Join strips on short ends to make one long strip; press seams open. Subcut strip into two 69½" F strips and two 59½" G strips.

Step 3. Cut nine 2¼" by fabric width binding strips black novelty print.

Step 4. Cut (13) 2½" by fabric width strips each gold mottled (B) and red tonal (C).

Step 5. Cut seven 4½" by fabric width strips red tonal. Join strips on short ends to make one long strip; press seams open. Subcut strip into two 72½" H strips and two 59½" I strips.

Step 6. Cut four 4½" by fabric width strips ornament print; subcut strips into (34) 4½" D squares.

Step 7. Cut nine 2½" by fabric width strips green mottled; subcut strips into (136) 2½" E squares. Mark a diagonal line from corner to corner on the wrong side of each square.

Step 8. Cut four 6½" x 84" strips along the length of the coordinating stripe. Fold one strip to find the center and then find the closest whole motif to this center; fold the strip again, centering the motif. Repeat for all strips. Cut two 80½" J strips and two 79½" K strips with the designs centered. **Note:** *It is easier to fold the strips and cut them 40¼" and 39¾" to keep the designs centered. This makes the design end the same on each end of each strip.*

COMPLETING THE QUILT
Step 1. Sew a B strip to a C strip with right sides together along the length; press seams toward C strips. Repeat to make 13 strip sets.

Step 2. Subcut the strip sets into (49) 9½" B-C units as shown in Figure 1.

Figure 1

Step 3. Referring to Figure 2, place an E square right sides together on opposite corners of D; stitch on the marked line. Trim seams to ¼" and press E to the right side.

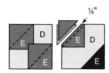

Figure 2

Step 4. Repeat Step 3 with two more E squares on the remaining corners of D referring to Figure 3 to complete a D-E unit. Repeat to make 34 D-E units.

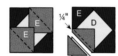

Figure 3

Step 5. Join four A squares with five B-C units to make a block row referring to Figure 4; press seams away from A. Repeat to make five block rows.

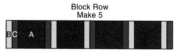

Figure 4

Step 6. Join four B-C units with five D-E units to make an X sashing row as shown in Figure 5; press seams toward the B-C units. Repeat to make three X sashing rows.

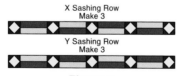

Figure 5

Step 7. Repeat Step 6 to make three Y sashing rows, again referring to Figure 5.

Step 8. Join the block rows with the X and Y sashing rows referring to the Placement Diagram

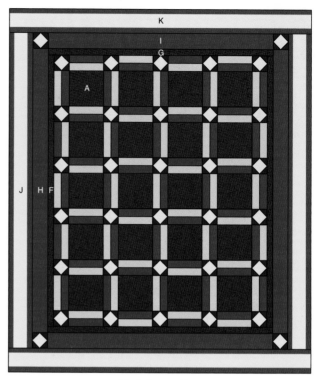

Christmas Fun
Placement Diagram
79" x 92"

for positioning of the X and Y sashing rows; press seams toward the block rows.

Step 9. Sew an F strip to opposite long sides and G strips to the top and bottom of the pieced center; press seams toward F and G strips.

Step 10. Sew H strips to opposite long sides of the pieced center; press seams toward H strips.

Step 11. Sew a D-E unit to each end of each I strip; press seams toward the I strips.

Step 12. Sew the D-E-I strips to the top and bottom of the pieced center; press seams toward the D-E-I strips.

Step 13. Sew J strips to opposite long sides and K strips to the top and bottom of the pieced center; press seams toward J and K strips. **Note:** *If your stripe has a definite up-and-down design, position strips with the correct directional orientation.*

Step 14. Quilt and bind referring to Completing Your Quilt on page 173. ❖

Christmas Snowballs

Design by **RUTH M. SWASEY**

Mix your scraps with your favorite Christmas prints in this bed-size quilt.

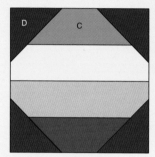

Pieced Snowball
8" x 8" Block
Make 40

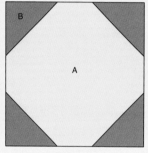

Snowball
8" x 8" Block
Make 40

PROJECT SPECIFICATIONS

Skill Level: Beginner
Quilt Size: 78½" x 94½"
Block Size: 8" x 8"
Number of Blocks: 80

MATERIALS

- 40 (2½"-wide) fabric-width C strips assorted Christmas prints
- 1½ yards total medium green prints
- 1½ yards cream poinsettia print
- 2⅛ yards dark green print
- 2½ yards cream snowflake print
- Backing 85" x 101"
- Batting 85" x 101"
- All-purpose thread to match fabrics
- Quilting thread
- Basic sewing tools and supplies

CUTTING

Step 1. Cut (10) 8½" by fabric width strips cream snowflake print; subcut strips into (40) 8½" A squares.

Step 2. Cut 14 total 3½" by fabric width strips medium green prints; subcut strips into (160) 3½" B squares. Draw a diagonal line from corner to corner on the wrong side of each square.

Step 3. Cut (14) 3½" by fabric width strips dark green print; subcut strips into (160) 3½" D squares. Draw a diagonal line from corner to corner on the wrong side of each square.

Step 4. Cut nine 2¼" by fabric width strips dark green print for binding.

Step 5. Cut (16) 3" by fabric width strips cream poinsettia print. Join strips on short ends to make one long strip; press seams open. Subcut strip into two strips each as follows: 80½" E, 69½" F, 90" G and 79" H.

COMPLETING THE SNOWBALL BLOCKS

Step 1. Referring to Figure 1, place a B square on each corner of A; stitch on the marked lines.

Figure 1   **Figure 2**   **Figure 3**

Step 2. Carefully trim ¼" beyond the stitched line, keeping the A-B layered waste units together as shown in Figure 2; press B to the right side to complete one Snowball block. Repeat to make 40 Snowball blocks.

Step 3. Stitch along the diagonal of 72 trimmed A-B waste units as shown in Figure 3; press open with seam toward B. Set aside for borders.

COMPLETING THE PIECED SNOWBALL BLOCKS

Step 1. Join four C strips with right sides together along length; press seams in one direction. Repeat to make 10 C strip sets.

Step 2. Subcut the C strip sets into (40) 8½" C units as shown in Figure 4.

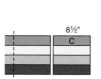

| Figure 4 | Figure 5 | Figure 6 |

Step 3. Referring to Figure 5, place a D square on each corner of a C unit; stitch on the marked lines.

Step 4. Carefully trim ¼" beyond the stitched line, keeping the C-D layered waste units together as shown in Figure 6; press D to the right side to complete one Pieced Snowball block. Repeat to make 40 Pieced Snowball blocks.

Step 5. Stitch along the diagonal of 72 trimmed C-D waste units as shown in Figure 7; press open with seam toward D. Set aside for borders.

Figure 7

COMPLETING THE QUILT

Step 1. Join four each Snowball and Pieced Snowball blocks to make a row; press seams toward the Snowball blocks. Repeat to make 10 rows.

Step 2. Join the rows referring to the Placement Diagram for positioning of blocks; press seams in one direction.

Christmas Snowballs
Placement Diagram
78½" x 94½"

Step 3. Sew an E strip to opposite long sides and F strips to the top and bottom of the pieced center; press seams toward the E and F strips.

Step 4. Sew an A-B unit to a C-D unit to make a border unit as shown in Figure 8; press seams in one direction. Repeat to make 72 border units.

Figure 8

Step 5. Join 19 border units to make a side strip; press seams in one direction. Repeat to make two side strips. Trim strips to 85½" and sew to opposite sides of the pieced center; press seams toward E strips.

Step 6. Join 17 border units to make a top strip; press seams in one direction. Repeat to make the bottom strip. Trim strips to 74" and sew to the top and bottom of the pieced center; press seams toward F strips.

Step 7. Sew G strips to opposite long sides and H strips to the top and bottom of the pieced center; press seams toward G and H strips.

Step 8. Quilt and bind referring to Completing your quilt on page 173. ❖

'Twas the Night Before Christmas

Design by **LUCY A. FAZELY & MICHAEL L. BURNS**

Wait for Santa's visit tucked under this warm and comfy quilt.

PROJECT SPECIFICATIONS

Skill Level: Intermediate
Quilt Size: 82" x 90"
Block Size: 12" x 12"
Number of Blocks: 25

MATERIALS

- ⅛ yard gray print
- ⅛ yard each 8 bright fabrics for lightbulbs
- ⅛ yard tan dot tonal
- ¼ yard brown tonal
- ⅓ yard gold swirl tonal
- ⅓ yard medium green print
- ⅝ yard white tonal
- ⅝ yard light green print
- 1⅛ yards brown/rust print
- 1⅝ yards gold star tonal
- 1⅞ yards dark green print
- 2⅝ yards dark blue print
- Backing 88" x 96"
- Batting 88" x 96"
- All-purpose thread to match fabrics
- Clear nylon monofilament
- Quilting thread
- 1 yard fusible web
- Removable fabric marker
- Basic sewing tools and supplies

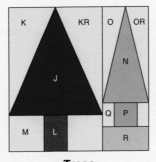

Trees
12" x 12" Block
Make 13

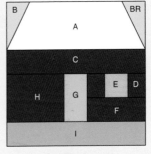

House
12" x 12" Block
Make 12

CUTTING

Step 1. Prepare templates using pattern pieces given.

Step 2. Cut four 4½" by fabric width strips white tonal; cut 12 A pieces from the strips referring to Figure 1.

Step 3. Cut one 4½" by fabric width strip gold star tonal; fold the strip in half across the width with wrong sides together. Cut 12 each B and BR pieces from the layered strip, again referring to Figure 1.

Step 4. Cut two 8½" by fabric width strips gold star tonal; place strips wrong sides together. Cut 13 each O and OR pieces from the layered strip, again referring to Figure 1. Cut (26) 1½" x 2½" Q rectangles from the remainder of the strips.

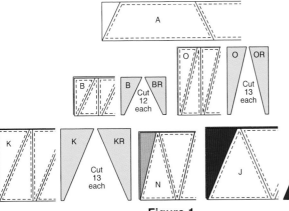

Figure 1

Step 5. Cut two 9½" by fabric width strips gold star tonal; place strips wrong sides together and cut 13 each K and KR pieces from the layered strip, again referring to Figure 1.

Step 6. Cut three 3½" by fabric width strips gold star tonal; subcut strips into (26) 3½" M squares.

Step 7. Cut two 5½" by fabric width strips brown/rust print; subcut strips into (12) 4½" H rectangles.

Step 8. Cut one 12½" by fabric width strip brown/rust print; subcut strip into (12) 2½" C rectangles.

Step 9. Cut one 5½" by fabric width strip brown/rust print; subcut strip into (12) 2½" F rectangles.

Step 10. Cut two 2½" by fabric width strips brown/rust print; subcut strips into (24) 2" D rectangles.

Step 11. Cut one 2½" by fabric width strip gold swirl tonal; subcut strip into (12) 2½" E squares.

Step 12. Cut one 4½" by fabric width strip gold swirl tonal; subcut strip into (12) 2½" G rectangles.

Step 13. Cut one 12½" strip light green print; subcut strip into (12) 2½" I rectangles.

Step 14. Cut one 4½" by fabric width strip light green print; subcut strip into (13) 2½" R rectangles.

Step 15. Cut two 9½" by fabric width strips dark green print; cut 13 J pieces from the strips, again referring to Figure 1.

Step 16. Cut six 2½" by fabric width S strips dark green print. Join strips on short ends to make one long strip; press seams open. Subcut strip into four 60½" S strips.

Step 17. Cut seven 3½" by fabric width strips dark green print. Join strips on short ends to make one long strip; press seams open. Subcut strip into two 68½" T strips and two 66½" U strips.

Step 18. Cut one 8½" by fabric width strip medium green print; cut 13 N pieces from the strip, again referring to Figure 1.

Step 19. Cut one 3½" by fabric width strip brown tonal; subcut strip into (13) 2½" L rectangles.

Step 20. Cut one 2½" by fabric width strip tan dot; subcut strip into (13) 2½" P squares.

Step 21. Cut eight 8½" by fabric width strips dark blue print. Join strips on short ends to make one long strip; press seams open. Subcut strip into two 74½" V strips and two 82½" W strips.

Step 22. Cut nine 2¼" by fabric width strips dark blue print for binding.

Step 23. Trace the lightbulb and base onto the paper side of the fusible web referring to patterns for number to cut; cut out shapes, leaving a margin around each one.

Step 24. Fuse the base shapes onto the wrong side of the gray print and five lightbulb shapes onto the wrong side of each of the bright fabrics. Cut out shapes on traced lines; remove paper backing.

'Twas the Night Before Christmas
Placement Diagram
82" x 90"

COMPLETING HOUSE BLOCKS

Step 1. To piece one House block, sew B and BR to A as shown in Figure 2 to make a roof unit; press seams toward B and BR.

Figure 2   **Figure 3**

Step 2. Sew D to opposite sides of E and add F to make a window unit as shown in Figure 3; press seams toward D and then F.

Step 3. Sew G to H to make a door unit as shown in Figure 4; press seam toward H.

Figure 4   **Figure 5**

Step 4. Join the window and door units as shown in Figure 5; press seams toward the G-H unit.

Step 5. Join the roof, window/door unit with C and I strips to complete one House block as shown in Figure 6; press seams toward C and I strips. Repeat to make 12 House blocks.

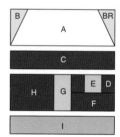

Figure 6

COMPLETING TREES BLOCKS

Step 1. Sew K and KR to J as shown in Figure 7; press seams toward K and KR.

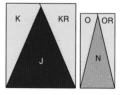

Figure 7

Step 2. Sew O and OR to N, again referring to Figure 7; press seams toward O and OR.

Step 3. Sew M to opposite sides of L as shown in Figure 8; press seams toward L.

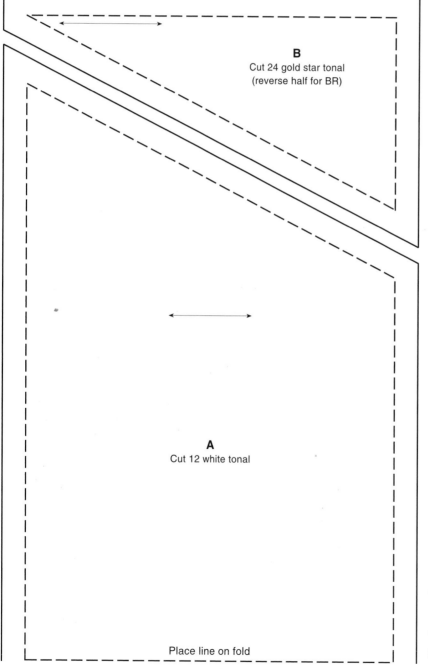

B
Cut 24 gold star tonal
(reverse half for BR)

A
Cut 12 white tonal

Place line on fold

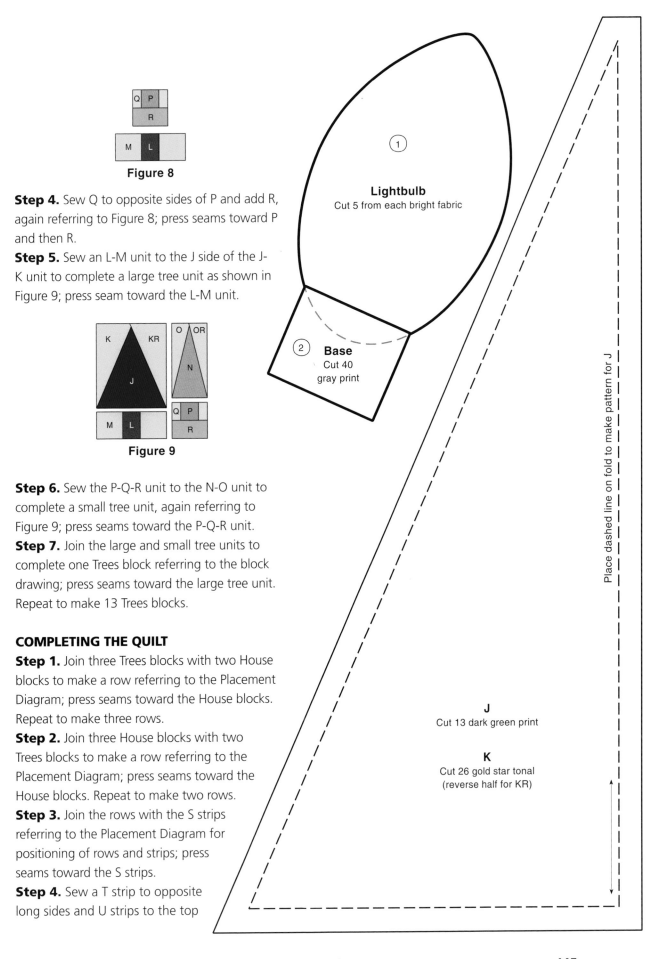

Figure 8

Step 4. Sew Q to opposite sides of P and add R, again referring to Figure 8; press seams toward P and then R.

Step 5. Sew an L-M unit to the J side of the J-K unit to complete a large tree unit as shown in Figure 9; press seam toward the L-M unit.

Figure 9

Step 6. Sew the P-Q-R unit to the N-O unit to complete a small tree unit, again referring to Figure 9; press seams toward the P-Q-R unit.

Step 7. Join the large and small tree units to complete one Trees block referring to the block drawing; press seams toward the large tree unit. Repeat to make 13 Trees blocks.

COMPLETING THE QUILT

Step 1. Join three Trees blocks with two House blocks to make a row referring to the Placement Diagram; press seams toward the House blocks. Repeat to make three rows.

Step 2. Join three House blocks with two Trees blocks to make a row referring to the Placement Diagram; press seams toward the House blocks. Repeat to make two rows.

Step 3. Join the rows with the S strips referring to the Placement Diagram for positioning of rows and strips; press seams toward the S strips.

Step 4. Sew a T strip to opposite long sides and U strips to the top

Lightbulb
Cut 5 from each bright fabric

Base
Cut 40
gray print

Place dashed line on fold to make pattern for J

J
Cut 13 dark green print

K
Cut 26 gold star tonal
(reverse half for KR)

and bottom of the pieced center; press seams toward the T and U strips.

Step 5. Sew a V strip to opposite long sides and W strips to the top and bottom of the pieced center; press seams toward the V and W strips.

Step 6. Using the removable fabric marker, draw a random line around the outer quilt border, referring to the Placement Diagram and quilt photo.

Step 7. Using gray all-purpose thread and a close, narrow zigzag stitch, stitch along the marked line.

Step 8. Randomly place the colored lightbulb shapes along the stitched "wire" line; iron in place. Fuse a base piece over the bottom end of each fused lightbulb shape.

Step 9. Using clear nylon monofilament and a close machine-zigzag stitch, stitch around lightbulb and base shapes.

Step 10. Finish the quilt referring to Completing Your Quilt on page 173. ❖

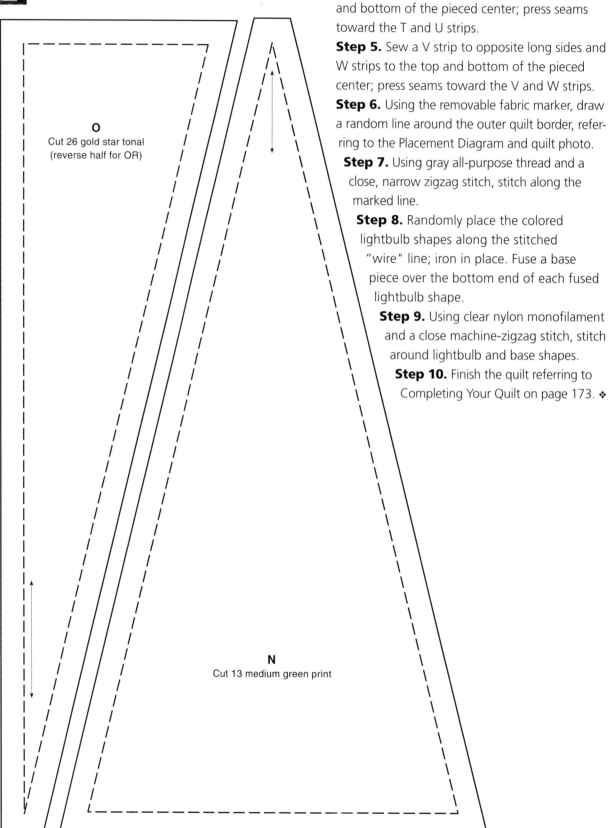

O
Cut 26 gold star tonal
(reverse half for OR)

N
Cut 13 medium green print

Scrappy Red Christmas

Design by **RUTH M. SWASEY**

A variety of red fabrics combine with white solid to make a striking Christmas quilt.

PROJECT SPECIFICATIONS

Skill Level: Intermediate
Quilt Size: 93½" x 110½"
Block Sizes: 12" x 12"
Number of Blocks: 50

MATERIALS

- 20 strips 5" by fabric width red fabrics
- 30 strips 6" by fabric width red fabrics
- 3½ yards red tonal
- 7 yards white solid
- Backing 100" x 117"
- Batting 100" x 117"
- All-purpose thread to match fabrics
- Quilting thread
- Rotary ruler with 45-degree-angle line
- Basic sewing tools and supplies

CUTTING

Step 1. Trim the 6" by fabric width strips to 5⅜"; subcut each strip into four 5⅜" squares. Cut each square in half on one diagonal to make eight A triangles to total 240 A triangles.

Step 2. Trim the 5" by fabric width strips to 4⅝"; subcut each strip into four 4⅝" squares.

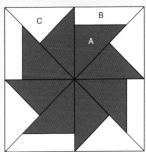

Pinwheel
12" x 12" Block
Make 30

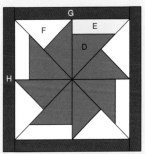

Framed Pinwheel
12" x 12" Block
Make 20

Cut each square in half on one diagonal to make eight D triangles to total 160 D triangles.

Step 3. Cut six 6⅞" by fabric width strips white solid; subcut strips into (120) 2" B rectangles. Cut one end of each rectangle at a 45-degree angle as shown in Figure 1.

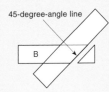

45-degree-angle line

B

Figure 1

Step 4. Cut six 7¼" by fabric width strips white solid; subcut strips into (30) 7¼" squares. Cut each square on both diagonals to make 120 C triangles.

Step 5. Cut four 5⅞" by fabric width strips white solid; subcut strips into (80) 1¾" E rectangles. Cut one end of each rectangle at a 45-degree angle, again referring to Figure 1.

Step 6. Cut one 8" by fabric width strip white solid; subcut strip into two 8" squares. Cut each square in half on one diagonal to make four K triangles.

Step 7. Trim the remainder of the 8"-wide strip white solid to 6¼"; subcut strip into four 6¼" squares.

Step 8. Cut three 6¼" by fabric width strips white solid; subcut strips into (16) 6¼" squares. Cut each of these squares and those cut in Step 7 on both diagonals to make 80 F triangles.

Step 9. Cut three 15⅜" by fabric width strips white solid; subcut strips into five 15⅜" squares. Cut each square on both diagonals to make 18 I triangles.

Step 10. Cut (10) 2⅝" by fabric width strips white solid. Join strips on short ends to make one long strip; press seams open. Subcut strip into two 102½" L strips and two 89¾" M strips.

Step 11. Cut four 5½" by fabric width strips white solid; subcut strips into (23) 5½" squares. Cut each square on both diagonals to make 92 N triangles.

Step 12. Cut two 10½" by fabric width strips red tonal; subcut strips into (40) 1½" G strips.

Step 13. Cut three 12½" by fabric width strips red tonal; subcut strips into (58) 1½" H strips.

Step 14. Cut one 14½" by fabric width strip red tonal; subcut strip into (22) 1½" J strips.

Step 15. Cut four 5½" by fabric width strips red tonal; subcut strips into (22) 5½" squares and two 5⅛" x 5⅛" squares. Cut each 5½" square on both diagonals to make 88 O triangles and each 5⅛" square in half on one diagonal to make four P triangles.

Step 16. Cut (10) 2¼" by fabric width strips red tonal for binding.

COMPLETING THE PINWHEEL BLOCKS

Step 1. To complete one block, sew B to A as

shown in Figure 2; press seam toward A. Repeat to make four matching A-B units.

Figure 2   **Figure 3**

Step 2. Select four A pieces to match those used in the A-B units. Sew C to A as shown in Figure 3; press seam toward A. Repeat to make four A-C units.

Step 3. Sew an A-B unit to an A-C unit to complete a block quarter as shown in Figure 4; press seams toward the A-B unit. Repeat to make four quarter units.

Figure 4   **Figure 5**

Step 4. Join two quarter units to make a row referring to Figure 5; press seam toward the A-C unit. Repeat to make two rows.

Step 5. Join the rows to complete one Pinwheel block referring to the block drawing; press seam in one direction. Repeat to make 30 blocks.

COMPLETING THE FRAMED PINWHEEL BLOCKS

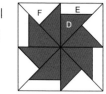

Figure 6

Step 1. Complete 20 pinwheel centers referring to Completing the Pinwheel Blocks and Figure 6 and using D, E and F pieces.

Step 2. To complete one Framed Pinwheel block, sew G to two opposite sides and H to the remaining sides of the pieced center referring to the block drawing; press seams toward G and H strips. Repeat to make 20 blocks.

COMPLETING THE QUILT

Step 1. Sew an H strip to one side of I as shown in Figure 7; press seams toward H.

Step 2. Sew J to the remaining side of I, aligning

one end with the square end of H, again referring to Figure 7; press seams toward J.

Figure 7

Step 3. Trim H and J ends even with I as shown in Figure 8 to complete an H-I-J unit; repeat to make 18 units.

Figure 8   **Figure 9**

Step 4. Center and sew J to the long side of each K triangle to complete four J-K units as shown in Figure 9; press seams toward J.

Step 5. Trim the J strips even with the edges of K, again referring to Figure 9.

Step 6. Arrange and join the pieced blocks in diagonal rows with the H-I-J and J-K triangle units as shown in Figure 10; press seams in adjoining rows in opposite directions.

Figure 10

Step 7. Join the rows to complete the pieced center; press seams in one direction.

Step 8. Sew L strips to opposite long sides and M strips to the top and bottom of the pieced center; press seams toward L and M strips.

Scrappy Red Christmas
Placement Diagram
93½" x 110½"

Step 9. Join 21 N and 20 O triangles as shown in Figure 11 to complete the top strip; press seams toward N. Repeat to make the bottom strip.

Figure 11

Step 10. Center and sew the N-O strips to the top and bottom of the pieced center referring to the Placement Diagram; press seams toward M strips.

Step 11. Repeat Step 9 with 25 N and 24 O triangles to make a side strip; press seams toward N. Repeat to make two side strips.

Step 12. Sew the N-O strips to opposite sides of the pieced center referring to the Placement Diagram; press seams toward L strips.

Step 13. Sew a P triangle to each corner to complete the pieced top; press seams toward P triangles.

Step 14. Quilt and bind referring to Completing Your Quilt on page 173. ❖

Surrounded by Flakes

Design by **RHONDA L. TAYLOR**

Snowball and Snowflake blocks in black and white fabrics make a striking winter statement.

PROJECT SPECIFICATIONS

Skill Level: Beginner
Quilt Size: 84" x 96"
Block Size: 6" x 6"
Number of Blocks: 149

MATERIALS

- ½ yard white tonal
- ¾ yard white/black star print
- 1⅜ yards black-with-white dots
- 4¼ yards black-with-white stars
- 4½ yards white-with-black stars
- Backing 90" x 102"
- Batting 90" x 102"
- All-purpose thread to match fabrics
- Quilting thread
- 1¼ yards fusible web
- Basic sewing tools and supplies

CUTTING

Step 1. Cut (17) 6½" by fabric width strips white-with-black stars; subcut strips into (98) 6½" A squares.

Step 2. Cut (13) 2½" by fabric width strips white-with-black stars; subcut strips into (204) 2½" D

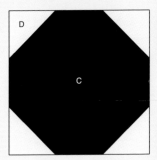

Black Snowball
6" x 6" Block
Make 51

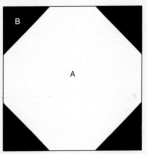

White Snowball
6" x 6" Block
Make 62

Snowflake
6" x 6" Block
Make 36

squares. Draw a diagonal line from corner to corner on the wrong side of each square.

Step 3. Cut (16) 2½" by fabric width strips black-with-white stars; subcut strips into (248) 2½" B squares. Draw a diagonal line from corner to corner on the wrong side of each square.

Step 4. Cut (14) 6½" by fabric width strips black-with-white stars; subcut strips into (79) 6½" C squares.

Step 5. Cut (14) 1" by fabric width strips white tonal. Join strips on short ends to make one long strip; press seams open. Subcut strip into two each 66½" E, 67½" F, 83½" I and 72½" J strips.

Step 6. Cut four 2½" by fabric width strips

black-with-white dots. Join strips on short ends to make one long strip; press seams open. Subcut strip into two 67½" G strips.

Step 7. Cut four 8½" by fabric width strips black-with-white dots. Join strips on short ends to make one long strip; press seams open. Subcut strip into two 71½" H strips.

Step 8. Cut nine 2¼" by fabric width strips white/black star print for binding.

Step 9. Trace snowflake and circle shapes onto the paper side of the fusible web as directed on each piece for number to cut. Cut out shapes, leaving a margin around each one.

Step 10. Fuse paper shapes to the wrong side of fabrics as directed on each piece for color and number to cut; cut out shapes on traced lines. Remove paper backing.

COMPLETING THE SNOWBALL BLOCKS

Step 1. Referring to Figure 1, place a B square on each corner of A; stitch on the marked lines.

Figure 1   **Figure 2**

Step 2. Trim seam allowance to ¼" and press B pieces to the right side to complete one White Snowball block referring to Figure 2. Repeat to make 62 blocks.

Figure 3

Step 3. Repeat Steps 1 and 2 with D on each corner of C to complete 51 Black Snowball blocks referring to Figure 3.

COMPLETING THE SNOWFLAKE BLOCKS

Step 1. Fold the remaining A squares in half vertically and horizontally and crease to mark the centers as shown in Figure 4.

Step 2. Fold each fused circle shape as in Step 1 and crease to mark the centers, again referring to Figure 4.

Figure 4   **Figure 5**

Step 3. Center a circle shape on A using creased lines as guides as shown in Figure 5; fuse in place.

Step 4. Machine-appliqué circle shapes in place using a medium-width buttonhole stitch.

Step 5. Repeat Steps 1–4 to complete 36 Snowflake blocks.

COMPLETING THE QUILT

Step 1. Join blocks in rows with C squares as shown in Figure 6; press seams toward C squares and away from White Snowball blocks.

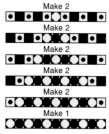

Figure 6

Step 2. Join rows to complete the pieced center referring to the Placement Diagram for positioning; press seams in one direction.

Step 3. Sew E strips to opposite long sides and F strips to the top and bottom of the pieced center; press seams toward E and F strips.

Step 4. Repeat Step 5 with G, H, I and J strips referring to the Placement Diagram; press seams toward each newly added strip before adding another strip.

Step 5. Join seven each White Snowball and Black Snowball blocks to make a side strip referring to the Placement Diagram; press seams in one direction. Repeat to make two side strips.

Step 6. Sew the side strips to opposite long sides of the pieced center; press seams toward strips.

Step 7. Join six each White Snowball and Black Snowball blocks to make the top strip; press seams in one direction. Add a C square to each end; press seam away from C. Repeat to make the bottom strip.

Step 8. Sew the pieced strips to the top and bottom of the pieced center referring to the Placement Diagram; press seams toward strips.

Step 9. Arrange and fuse six snowflake shapes on each H strip referring to the Placement Diagram for positioning to complete the top. ***Note:*** *The snowflake shapes will be secured in place during the quilting process.*

Step 10. Quilt and bind referring to Completing Your Quilt on page 173. ❖

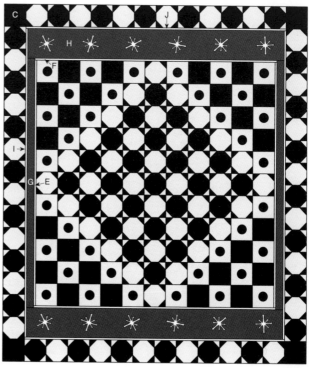

Surrounded by Flakes
Placement Diagram
84" x 96"

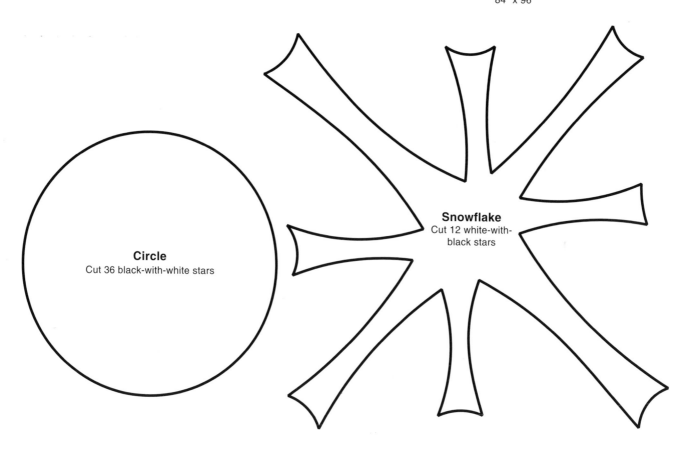

Circle
Cut 36 black-with-white stars

Snowflake
Cut 12 white-with-black stars

Oh Christmas Tree

Design by **LINDA MILLER**

Create this fun folk-art tree quilt sampler.

PROJECT SPECIFICATIONS

Skill Level: Advanced

Quilt Size: 75½" x 87½"

Block Sizes: 24" x 24", 16½" x 14", 12" x 23½",
12" x 12", 17" x 11½", 5" x 14", 12½" x 29",
12½" x 12½", 12½" x 30", 12" x 13", 18" x
24", 18" x 17" and 18" x 17½"

Number of Blocks: 13

MATERIALS

- ⅓ yard cream print
- ⅔ yard cream/red plaid
- 1 yard cream Osnaburg
- Large variety cream, tan, red, green and
  brown homespun scraps
- 3 yards green/cream check
- Backing 82" x 94"
- Batting 82" x 94"
- All-purpose thread to match fabrics
- Quilting thread
- 2 skeins black embroidery floss
- 5 (¼") black buttons
- 12 (⅜") red buttons
- 3 (½") wooden buttons
- Water-erasable marker or pencil
- Basic sewing tools and supplies

CUTTING FLYING GEESE BLOCK

Step 1. Cut four 10" x 5¼" A rectangles each
two different green homespuns.

Step 2. Cut two 5¼" by fabric width strips
cream/red plaid; subcut strips into (16) 5¼" B

squares. Mark a diagonal line from corner to corner on the wrong side of each square.

Step 3. Cut six 4¼" x 5½" C rectangles cream/
red plaid.

Step 4. Cut one 5½" x 13" E strip cream/
red plaid.

Step 5. Cut four 2½" x 5½" D rectangles
brown homespun.

COMPLETING FLYING GEESE BLOCK

Step 1. Referring to Figure 1, place
B on one end of A; stitch on the
marked line. Trim seam allowance to
¼"; press B to the right side.

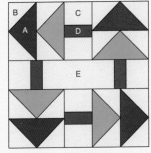

Flying Geese
24" x 24" Block
Make 1

Figure 1

Step 2. Repeat Step 1 on the remaining end of A to complete an A-B unit
as shown in Figure 2. Repeat to make eight
A-B units.

Figure 2   **Figure 3**

Step 3. Sew D between two C rectangles
to complete a C-D unit as shown in Figure 3;
press seam toward D. Repeat to make two
C-D units.

Step 4. Join one A-B unit of each green homespun

as shown in Figure 4; press seam in one direction. Repeat to make four joined A-B units.

 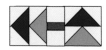

Figure 4   **Figure 5**

Step 5. Join two joined A-B units with a C-D unit to make a row as shown in Figure 5; press seam toward C-D unit. Repeat to make two rows.

Step 6. Sew D to each end of E and add C to complete the C-D-E unit as shown in Figure 6; press seams toward D.

Step 7. Sew the C-D-E unit between the two rows referring to Figure 7 to complete the Flying Geese block; press seams toward C-D-E.

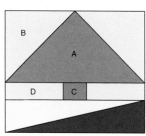

Figure 6   **Figure 7**

CUTTING TREE 1 BLOCK

Step 1. Cut one 17" x 8¾" A rectangle green/cream check.

Step 2. Cut two 8¾" x 8¾" B squares red homespun. Mark a diagonal line from corner to corner on the wrong side of each square.

Step 3. Cut one 2½" x 3" C rectangle tan homespun.

Step 4. Cut two 2½" x 7½" D rectangles red homespun.

Step 5. Cut one 4¼" x 19" rectangle each cream and green homespuns; cut each rectangle from one corner to the other to make E triangles as shown in Figure 8. Discard one triangle of each fabric.

Tree 1
16½" x 14" Block
Make 1

Figure 8

COMPLETING TREE 1 BLOCK

Step 1. Complete one A-B unit referring to Steps 1 and 2 for Completing Flying Geese Block and Figure 9.

Figure 9   **Figure 10**

Step 2. Sew C between two D pieces to complete the C-D unit as shown in Figure 10; press seams toward D.

Step 3. Sew E to E as shown in Figure 11; press seam in one direction.

Figure 11   **Figure 12**

Step 4. Join the A-B, C-D and E units to complete the Tree 1 block referring to Figure 12.

CUTTING TREE 2 BLOCK

Step 1. Cut one 8½" x 18" A rectangle cream homespun.

Step 2. Cut one 3½" x 8½" J strip each cream/red plaid and red homespun.

Step 3. Cut one 2½" x 24" K strip each green and red homespuns.

Step 4. Prepare templates for Tree 2 pieces using patterns given; cut as directed on each piece.

COMPLETING TREE 2 BLOCK

Step 1. Sew a J strip to the short sides of A; press seams toward J strips.

Step 2. Sew K strips to opposite long sides of the A-J unit; press seams toward K strips.

Step 3. Sew B to C along one short side as marked on pattern; repeat with D and E, F and G,

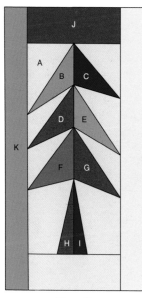

Tree 2
12" x 23½" Block
Make 1

and H and I referring to Figure 13; press seams open.

Step 4. Turn under edges of each unit ¼" all around.

Step 5. Arrange pieces on the A rectangle referring to the block drawing and appliqué in place.

Figure 13

Tree 3
12" x 12" Block
Make 1

CUTTING TREE 3 BLOCK

Step 1. Make two copies of the tree paper-piecing pattern. Cut one copy apart on solid lines to make templates.

Step 2. Using the templates, cut pieces as directed on pattern for color, adding at least ¼" all around each piece when cutting.

Step 3. Cut 2"-wide homespun strips as follows: one each 6½" A and 12½" E and two each 8" B, 9½" C and 11" D.

COMPLETING TREE 3 BLOCK

Step 1. Pin piece 1 onto the unmarked side of the paper pattern in the area marked 1.

Step 2. Referring to Figure 14, pin piece 2 right sides together on the piece 2 side of piece 1.

Step 3. Turn the paper over and stitch on the line between pieces 1 and 2 as shown in Figure 15.

Figure 14   **Figure 15**

Step 4. Trim seam allowance to ¼"; flip piece 2 to the right side and press flat.

Step 5. Continue adding pieces in numerical order to complete the block center as shown in Figure 16; trim along outside solid line.

Step 6. Sew A to the top edge of the pieced center as shown in Figure 17; press seam toward A.

Figure 16   **Figure 17**   **Figure 18**

Step 7. Continue adding pieces around the pieced center in alphabetical order referring to Figure 18, pressing seams toward newly added strips as you sew to complete the Tree 3 block.

CUTTING TREE 4 BLOCK

Step 1. Cut one 17½" x 12" A rectangle red homespun.

Step 2. Cut three 9" x 3½" rectangles total green and cream homespuns. Fold each rectangle to

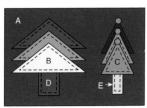

Tree 4
17" x 11½" Block
Make 1

mark the center of the long sides. Cut from the center to each opposite corner to make a B triangle as shown in Figure 19. Repeat to cut three B Osnaburg triangles.

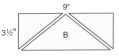

Figure 19   **Figure 20**

Step 3. Cut three 4" x 4" squares total green and red homespuns; fold each square to mark the center. Cut from the center to each opposite corner to make C triangles as shown in Figure 20. Repeat to cut three C Osnaburg triangles.

Step 4. Cut one 2" x 3" D rectangle each brown homespun and Osnaburg.

Step 5. Cut one 1¼" x 2½" E rectangle each cream homespun and Osnaburg.

COMPLETING TREE 4 BLOCK

Step 1. Layer each homespun triangle with a same-size Osnaburg triangle.

Step 2. Arrange and pin same-size layered tree triangles to A, overlapping triangles as shown in Figure 21, to make tree tops.

Step 3. Center and pin the D rectangle ¼" under the pinned B triangles, again referring to Figure 21; repeat with the E rectangle under the C triangles.

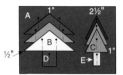 

Figure 21   **Figure 22**

Step 4. Stitch each shape in place ¼" from the edges, starting with D and E pieces and working from the top to the bottom of the tree on each treetop motif as shown in Figure 22.

Step 5. Sew a ½" wooden button to the tip of each C tree triangle to complete the block.

CUTTING TREE 5 BLOCK

Step 1. Cut one 5½" x 14½" A rectangle cream/red plaid.

Step 2. Cut five 3½" x 4½" B rectangles red homespun.

Step 3. Fold each B rectangle to find the center of the 3½" sides; cut from the center mark to each bottom corner to make B triangles as shown in Figure 23.

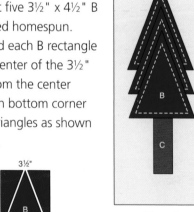

Tree 5
5" x 14" Block
Make 1

Figure 23

Step 4. Cut two 1" x 3" C rectangles brown homespun.

COMPLETING TREE 5 BLOCK

Step 1. Complete the block as for Tree 4 except layer two C pieces for trunk and offset single B triangles from top to bottom as shown in Figure 24.

Figure 24

CUTTING TREE 6 BLOCK

Step 1. Cut six 3" x 8" A rectangles from a variety of homespuns.

Step 2. Cut one 3⅜" x 3⅜" B square to match each A rectangle; cut each square in half on one diagonal to make two B triangles of each fabric.

Step 3. Cut six 3⅜" x 3⅜" C squares cream homespun; cut each square in half on one diagonal to make 12 C triangles.

Step 4. Cut two 5¾" x 8" D rectangles cream homespun.

Step 5. Cut one 3" x 15⅛" F rectangle green homespun; cut as shown in Figure 25. Discard small triangles.

Figure 25

Step 6. Cut two 3⅛" x 7⅞" G rectangles cream homespun; cut as shown in Figure 26 to make G and GR triangles. Discard one of each triangle.

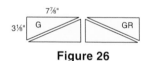

Figure 26

Step 7. Cut one 4½" x 13" H rectangle cream homespun.

Step 8. Cut one 2½" x 8" E rectangle brown homespun.

COMPLETING TREE 6 BLOCK

Step 1. Sew B to C to make a B-C unit as shown in Figure 27; repeat to make 12 B-C units. Press seams toward B.

Figure 27   **Figure 28**

Step 2. Sew two matching B-C units to A to complete one A-B-C unit as shown in Figure 28; repeat to make six A-B-C units. Press seams toward A.

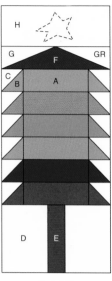

Tree 6
12½" x 29" Block
Make 1

Step 3. Join the six A-B-C units as shown in Figure 29; press seams in one direction.

Step 4. Sew G and GR to angled sides of F to complete an F-G unit as shown in Figure 30; press seams toward G and GR.

Figure 29

Figure 30

Step 5. Sew the F-G unit to the top of the A-B-C unit and add H as shown in Figure 31 to complete the treetop unit; press seams toward F-G and H.

Step 6. Sew E between two D rectangles; press seams toward E.

Step 7. Sew the D-E unit to the bottom of the treetop unit referring to Figure 32; press seam toward D-E unit.

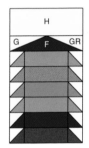

Figure 31

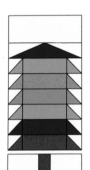

Figure 32

Step 8. Transfer the star pattern onto the H rectangle using the full-size pattern given.

Step 9. Using 6 strands of black embroidery floss, straight-stitch along the marked lines.

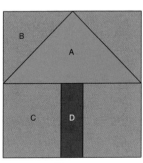

Tree 7
12½" x 12½" Block
Make 1

CUTTING TREE 7 BLOCK

Step 1. Cut one 6¾" x 13" A rectangle green homespun.

Step 2. Cut two 6¾" x 6¾" B squares tan homespun; mark a diagonal line from corner to corner on the wrong side of each square.

Step 3. Cut two 5¾" x 6¾" C rectangles tan homespun.

Step 4. Cut one 2½" x 6¾" D rectangle brown homespun.

COMPLETING TREE 7 BLOCK

Step 1. Step 1. Complete one A-B unit referring to Steps 1 and 2 for Completing Flying Geese Block and Figure 33.

Figure 33   **Figure 34**

Step 2. Sew D between two C pieces; press seams toward D.

Step 3. Sew the C-D unit to the A-B unit to complete the Tree 7 block as shown in Figure 34.

CUTTING TREE 8 BLOCK

Step 1. Cut one 9" x 24½" A rectangle cream print.

Step 2. Cut one 3" x 24½" B strip cream homespun.

Step 3. Cut one 3½" x 11½" C strip green homespun.

Step 4. Cut one 2" x 27½" D strip green homespun.

Step 5. Cut one 3½" x 13" E strip red homespun.

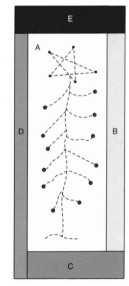

Tree 8
12½" x 30" Block
Make 1

COMPLETING TREE 8 BLOCK

Step 1. Sew B to one side of A; press seam toward B. Add C to the bottom, D to the opposite side and E to the top of the A-B unit referring to Figure 35; press seams toward C, D and E strips.

Step 2. Referring to Figure 36, mark a 17"-long wiggly line for the trunk on A; add six varying branches on each side of the trunk and a line at the bottom of the trunk for ground referring to the block drawing

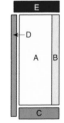

Figure 35

and quilt photo. Transfer the star pattern to the top of the trunk line using the full-size pattern given.

Step 3. Using 6 strands of black embroidery floss, straight-stitch along the marked lines.

Step 4. Sew a ⅜" red button to the end of each branch and a ¼" black button at each star point to complete the Tree 8 block.

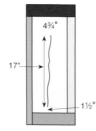

Figure 36

CUTTING TREE 9 BLOCK

Step 1. Cut one 13" x 9¼" A rectangle red homespun; cut as shown in Figure 37.

Figure 37

Step 2. Cut two 6¾" x 9⅝" B rectangles green homespun; cut as shown in Figure 38. Discard one each B and BR.

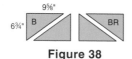

Figure 38

Step 3. Cut two 5¼" x 5" C rectangles cream/red plaid.

Step 4. Cut one 3" x 5" D rectangle brown homespun.

COMPLETING TREE 9 BLOCK

Step 1. Sew B and BR to A to complete an A-B unit as shown in Figure 39; press seams toward B and BR.

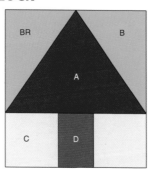

Tree 9
12" x 13" Block
Make 1

Figure 39   **Figure 40**

Step 2. Sew C to each side of D to complete a C-D unit; press seams toward D.

Step 3. Sew the C-D unit to the A-B unit to complete the Tree 9 block as shown in Figure 40; press seam toward the C-D unit.

CUTTING TREE 10 BLOCK

Step 1. Cut one 18½" x 24½" A rectangle cream homespun.

Step 2. Cut two 2" x 20" B strips each two tan homespuns.

Step 3. Cut two 2" x 20" C strips each two green homespuns.

Step 4. Cut two 2" x 23" D strips red homespun.

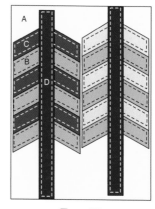

Tree 10
18" x 24" Block
Make 1

COMPLETING TREE 10 BLOCK

Step 1. Sew a B strip to a C strip with right sides together along the length to make a strip set; repeat to make an identical B-C strip set. Repeat with remaining strips to complete two more identical strip sets; press seams toward C strips.

Step 2. Measure over 2½" on the top edge of one end of one strip set and cut to the corner to make an angle as shown in Figure 41. Cut strips into six 5½" B-C units and six BR-CR units, again referring to Figure 41.

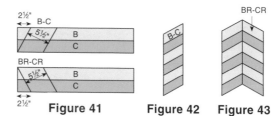

Figure 41   **Figure 42**   **Figure 43**

Step 3. Join three identical B-C units as shown in Figure 42; press seams in one direction. Repeat with three identical BR-CR units. Repeat to make a second set of joined B-C and BR-CR units.

Step 4. Join B-C and BR-CR units to complete a tree shape as shown in Figure 43; press seam open. Repeat to make two tree shapes.

Step 5. Arrange the tree shapes on A referring to the block drawing for positioning suggestions; machine-stitch ¼" from all edges to hold in place.

Step 6. Arrange the D strips on top through the centers of the tree shapes, varying placement from top to bottom as desired; stitch in place ¼" from edges all around to complete the Tree 10 block. *Note: If you prefer edges to be more ragged, cut Osnaburg pieces and layer with each strip when piecing.*

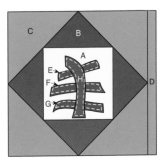

Tree 11
18" x 17" Block
Make 1

CUTTING TREE 11 BLOCK

Step 1. Cut one 9" x 9" A square cream homespun.

Step 2. Cut two 6⅞" x 6⅞" squares red homespun; cut each square in half on one diagonal to make four B triangles.

Step 3. Cut two 9⅜" x 9⅜" squares green homespun; cut each square in half on one diagonal to make four C triangles.

Step 4. Cut one 1½" x 17½" D strip green homespun.

Step 5. Prepare templates for tree shapes using patterns given; cut as directed on the shapes.

COMPLETING TREE 11 BLOCK

Step 1. Sew B to each side of A as shown in Figure 44; press seams toward B.

Step 2. Sew C to each side of the A-B unit, again referring to Figure 44; press seams toward C.

Figure 44

Step 3. Sew D to the side edge of the A-B-C unit referring to the block drawing; press seam toward D.

Step 4. Arrange the E, F and G pieces with the H piece on top on the A center of the pieced unit referring to the pattern and block drawing for positioning; stitch each shape in place ¼" from edges all around to complete the Tree 11 block.

Tree 12
18" x 17½" Block
Make 1

CUTTING TREE 12 BLOCK

Step 1. Cut one 12½" x 13½" A rectangle cream homespun.

Step 2. Cut one each green home-spun and Osnaburg rectangles in each of the following sizes: 9½" x 10" B; 4½" x 8" C, 2" x 4" D. Cut one 3" x 3" E square each brown homespun and Osnaburg.

Step 3. Layer a B homespun rectangle right side up on a same-size Osnaburg rectangle; pin to hold. Repeat for all C, D and E rectangles.

Step 4. Cut the layered B, C, D and E rectangles to make triangles as shown in Figure 45.

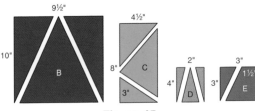

Figure 45

Step 5. Cut two 3½" x 13½" F strips green homespun.

Step 6. Cut two 2¾" x 18½" G strips green homespun.

COMPLETING TREE 12 BLOCK

Step 1. Sew F strips to opposite long sides of A; press seams toward F strips.

Step 2. Sew G strips to the top and bottom of A; press seams toward G strips.

Step 3. Arrange the B–E pieces on A, starting with E and then B, C and D pieces referring to the block drawing for positioning.

Step 4. When satisfied with placement, stitch ¼" from edges all around each piece.

CUTTING FOR THE QUILT

Step 1. Cut one 8" x 14½" AA rectangle red homespun.

Step 2. Cut one 24½" x 10½" BB rectangle cream homespun.

Step 3. Cut two 5½" x 23½" CC rectangles cream homespun.

Step 4. Cut one 6½" x 13½" DD rectangle cream print.

Step 5. Cut two 8½" x 72" EE strips and two 8½" x 76" FF strips along the length of the green/cream check.

Step 6. Cut 2¼"-wide bias strips green/cream check to total 340" for bias binding.

COMPLETING THE QUILT

Step 1. Sew AA to the Tree 1 block as shown in Figure 46; press seam toward AA. Sew the Flying Geese block to the top of the pieced unit, again referring to Figure 46; press seam toward the AA/block unit.

Figure 46

Step 2. Sew Tree 3 to Tree 4, stopping stitching 2" from the edge of Tree 3 as shown in Figure 47; press seam toward Tree 4.

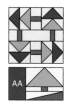

Figure 47

Step 3. Sew the Tree 2 block to the Tree 3/Tree 4 unit as shown in Figure 48; press seam toward Tree 2. Add BB to the top of the pieced unit, again referring to Figure 48; press seam toward BB.

Figure 48

Step 4. Sew the Tree 5 block between two CC rectangles to make a CC/block strip; press seams toward CC.

Step 5. Arrange the pieced sections as shown in Figure 49; join to complete a side row, completing the partial seam between the CC and Tree 3/Tree 4 section; press seams in one direction and toward the CC/block strip.

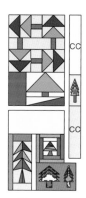

Figure 49

Step 6. Join the Tree 6, 7 and 8 blocks to make

Oh Christmas Tree
Placement Diagram
75½" x 87½"

the center row as shown in Figure 50; press seams in one direction.

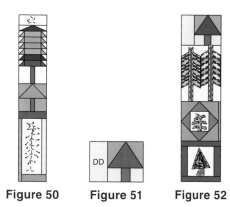

Figure 50   **Figure 51**   **Figure 52**

Step 7. Sew DD to Tree 9 as shown in Figure 51; press seam toward DD.

Step 8. Join the DD/Tree 9 unit with Trees 10, 11 and 12 to complete a right-side row as shown in Figure 52; press seams in one direction.

Step 9. Join the rows referring to the Placement Diagram to complete the pieced top.

Step 10. Sew EE strips to opposite long sides and FF strips to the top and bottom of the pieced center to complete the top; press seams toward EE and FF strips.

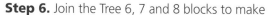

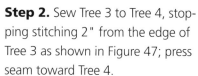

Holly Jolly Christmas Quilting ❖ **163**

Step 11. Using a water-erasable marker, write the messages (or use a computer font of your choice to create the letters) Oh Christmas Tree, How Lovely are Thy Branches, and JOY on the BB, CC and DD strips referring to the Placement Diagram.

Step 12. Using 6 strands of black embroidery floss, straight-stitch along all marked lines.

Step 13. Quilt and bind referring to Completing Your Quilt on page 173. ❖

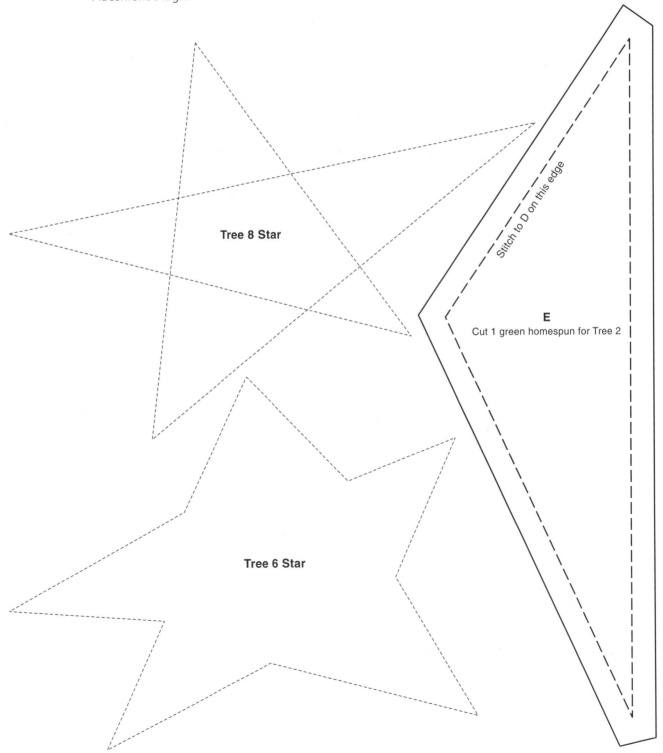

Tree 8 Star

Tree 6 Star

Stitch to D on this edge

E
Cut 1 green homespun for Tree 2

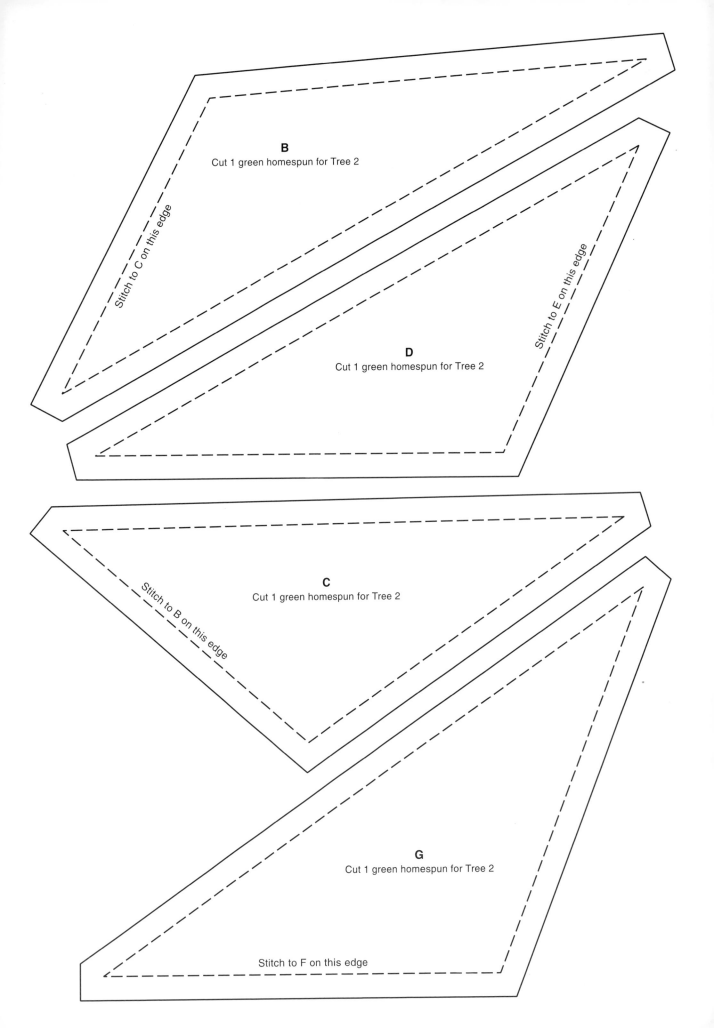

B
Cut 1 green homespun for Tree 2

Stitch to C on this edge

D
Cut 1 green homespun for Tree 2

Stitch to E on this edge

C
Cut 1 green homespun for Tree 2

Stitch to B on this edge

G
Cut 1 green homespun for Tree 2

Stitch to F on this edge

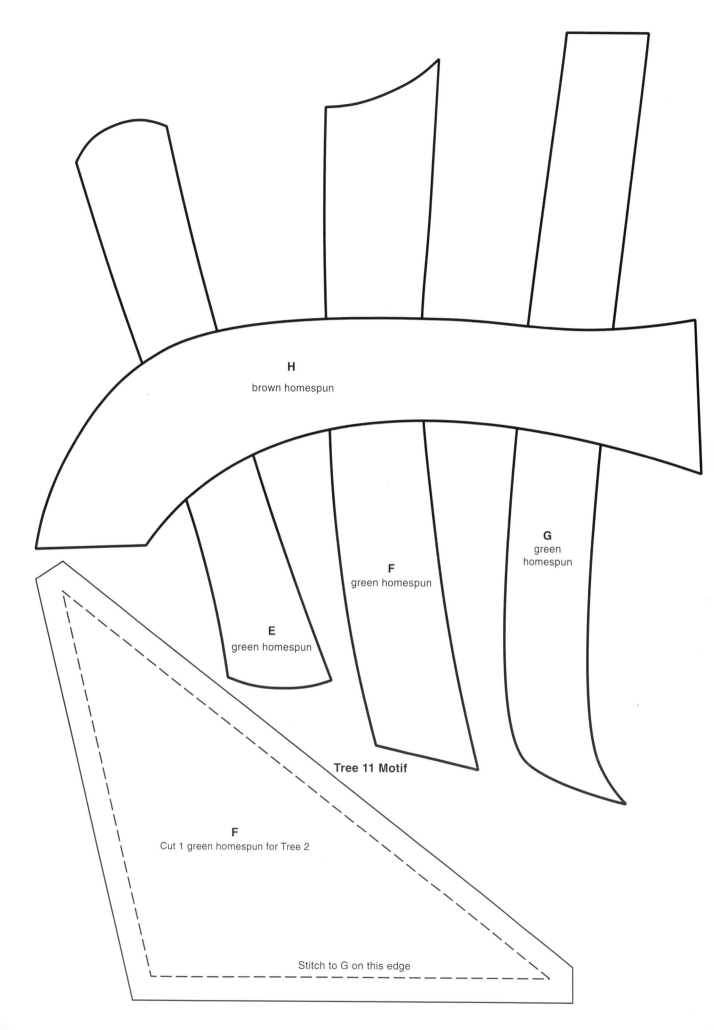

H

brown homespun

G

green homespun

F

green homespun

E

green homespun

Tree 11 Motif

F

Cut 1 green homespun for Tree 2

Stitch to G on this edge

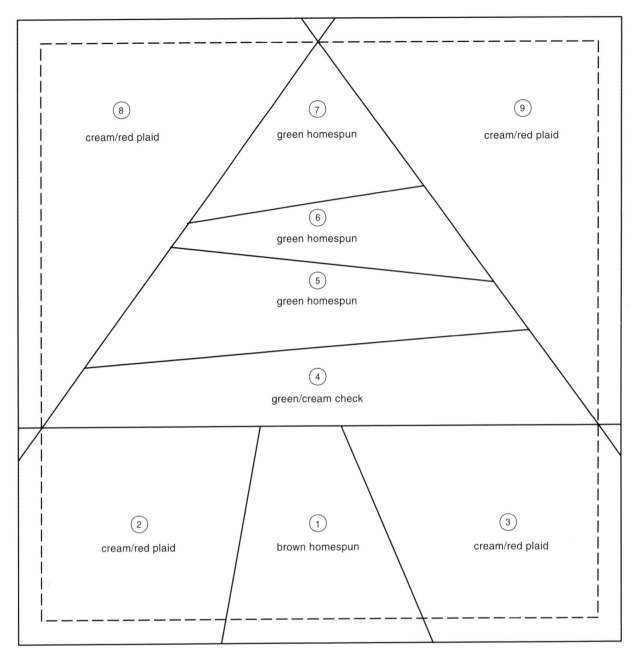

Tree 3 Paper-Piecing Pattern

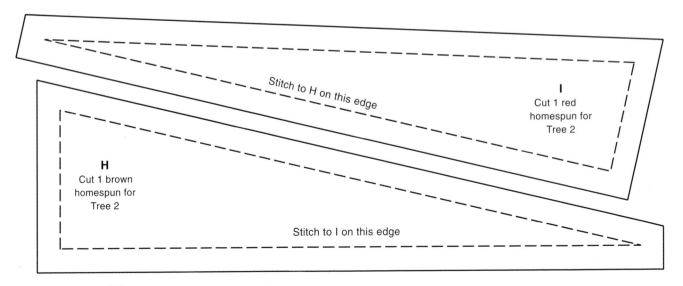

Tree-mendous Ornaments

Designs by **LINDA MILLER**

Decorate your cottage tree with a few of these ornaments.

Triangle Tree

PROJECT SPECIFICATIONS

Skill Level: Beginner
Ornament Size:
   Approximately
   5" x 6½"

MATERIALS

- Scraps plaid homespuns
- ⅛ yard Osnaburg
- All-purpose thread to match fabrics
- 2 yards green string
- Polyester fiberfill
- 5 (⅝") red buttons
- Basic sewing tools and supplies

INSTRUCTIONS

Step 1. Cut one Osnaburg and two plaid homespun 1½" x 3" rectangles for tree trunk.

Step 2. Layer the trunk pieces wrong sides together with Osnaburg between; stitch around sides and bottom using a ¼" seam allowance.

Step 3. Stuff polyester fiberfill between two of the layers; stitch to close opening.

Triangle Tree Ornament
Placement Diagram
Approximately 5" x 6½"

Step 4. Prepare the triangle template; cut as directed.

Step 5. Repeat Steps 2 and 3 with two plaid homespun and one Osnaburg triangle, leaving a 2" opening on the bottom edge for stuffing.

Step 6. Repeat Step 5 to make five stuffed triangles.

Step 7. Place the long side of one triangle between the tops of two triangles as shown in Figure 1; pin to hold.

Step 8. Place the long sides of the two bottom triangles from Step 7 between the two remaining triangles, again referring to Figure 1; pin to hold.

Step 9. Place one button on each side of center triangles at tips and stitch through all layers and the buttons on both sides as shown in Figure 2. Repeat with two bottom triangles.

Step 10. Center and insert the stuffed trunk piece between the two bottom triangles as shown in Figure 3; stitch to hold in place.

Step 11. Cut green string to make two equal lengths.

Step 12. Create a hanging loop and bow from one length of green string and attach to the top tree triangle with remaining button.

Step 13. Cut remaining green string in half and make two bows. Hand-stitch one bow to each

Figure 1

Figure 2

Figure 3

side at bottom of tree, just above trunk, to complete the ornament.

Layered Tree

PROJECT SPECIFICATIONS

Skill Level: Beginner
Ornament Size:
   Approximately
   6" x 5½"

Layered Tree Ornament
Placement Diagram
Approximately 6" x 5½"

MATERIALS

• Scraps plaid homespuns
• ⅛ yard Osnaburg
• All-purpose thread to match fabrics
• 1 yard green string
• Polyester fiberfill
• 2 (⅜") red buttons
• 1 red star button
• Spray bottle and water
• Toothbrush
• Basic sewing tools and supplies

INSTRUCTIONS

Step 1. Prepare templates for each layered-tree shape using patterns given; cut as directed.

Step 2. Cut one Osnaburg and two plaid homespun 1½" x 3" rectangles for tree trunk.

Step 3. Prepare tree trunk as in Steps 2 and 3 for the Triangle Tree.

Step 4. Pin an Osnaburg shape on the wrong side of each same-size plaid homespun shape.

Step 5. Layer the pinned shapes, starting with the largest and ending with the smallest as shown in Figure 4; using a ¼" seam allowance, stitch around each shape through all layers, starting with smallest shape in center.

Figure 4

Step 6. Spritz and brush to create a rag texture.

Step 7. Place the stitched unit wrong sides

together with the backing piece; stitch with a scant ¼" seam allowance, leaving a 2" opening in the bottom.

Step 8. Insert the trunk piece into the opening and baste to one edge.

Step 9. Stuff with polyester fiberfill and stitch the opening closed.

Step 10. Create a loop with approximately 1" ends at the top edge using green string. Sew the red star button to the tree top over loop ends.

Step 11. Sew two ⅜" red buttons to the center of the smallest triangle to complete the ornament.

Chenille Tree

PROJECT SPECIFICATIONS

Skill Level: Beginner
Ornament Size:
   Approximately 4½" x 6½"

Chenille Tree Ornament
Placement Diagram
Approximately 4½" x 6½"

MATERIALS

• Scraps plaid homespuns
• ¼ yard Osnaburg
• All-purpose thread to match fabrics
• Polyester fiberfill
• 7 (⅜") red buttons
• Spray bottle and water
• Toothbrush
• Fabric glue
• Basic sewing tools and supplies

INSTRUCTIONS

Step 1. Cut five 7" x 7" squares plaid homespun.

Step 2. Cut one 7" x 7" square Osnaburg.

Step 3. Cut two 1½" x 3" trunk pieces plaid homespun and one Osnaburg.

Step 4. Prepare tree trunk as in Steps 2 and 3 for the Triangle Tree.

Step 5. Layer four plaid squares and the Osnaburg square right side up on a flat surface, with the Osnaburg square centered in the layers.

Step 6. Stitch diagonal lines ½" apart to cover the entire square as shown in Figure 5.

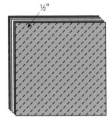

Figure 5

Step 7. Cut down the center between stitching lines through all except the bottom layer as shown in Figure 6.

Figure 6

Step 8. Spritz the square with water and brush with a toothbrush to fringe; let dry.

Step 9. Prepare a template for the Chenille tree; trace the tree shape on the right side of the remaining plaid homespun square.

Step 10. Place brushed squares wrong sides together with the traced backing square.

Step 11. Stitch on the marked line through all layers, leaving a 2" opening in the center on the bottom edge of the tree shape.

Step 12. Trim ¼" beyond stitching line as shown in Figure 7.

Step 13. Stuff with polyester fiberfill.

Step 14. Insert the trunk

Figure 7

piece into the opening and stitch the opening closed.

Step 15. Cut a 3" piece of the cutaway layered-and-stitched section, centering a line of stitching in the piece as shown in Figure 8; fold to make a loop.

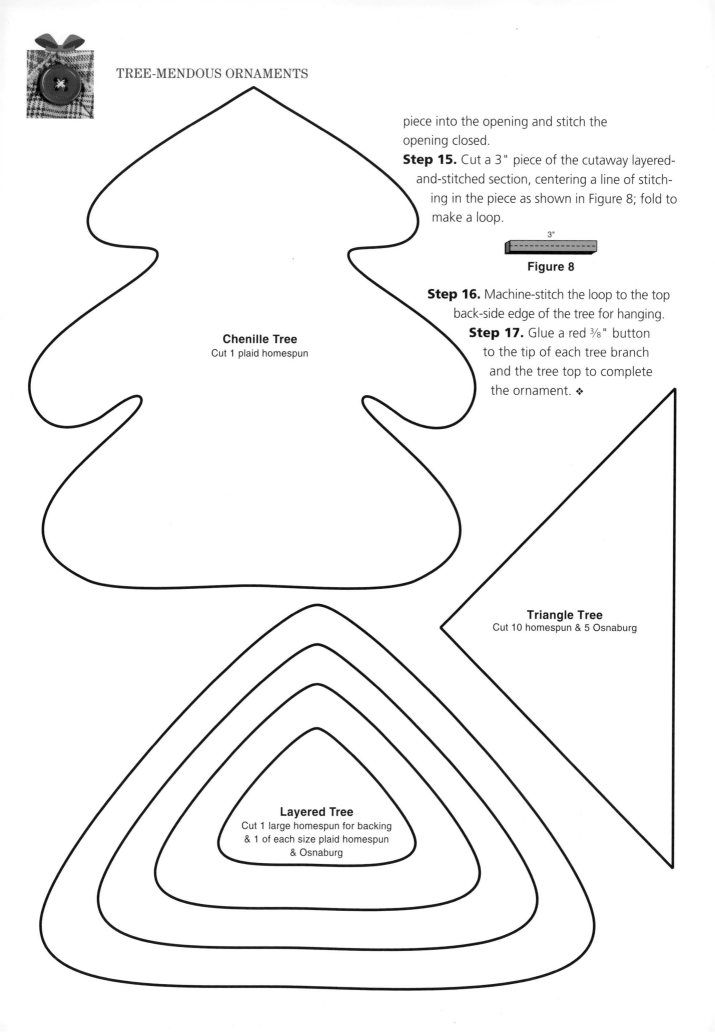

3"

Figure 8

Step 16. Machine-stitch the loop to the top back-side edge of the tree for hanging.

Step 17. Glue a red ⅜" button to the tip of each tree branch and the tree top to complete the ornament. ❖

Chenille Tree
Cut 1 plaid homespun

Triangle Tree
Cut 10 homespun & 5 Osnaburg

Layered Tree
Cut 1 large homespun for backing
& 1 of each size plaid homespun
& Osnaburg

General Instructions

COMPLETING YOUR QUILT

Marking the Top for Quilting

If you choose a fancy or allover design for quilting, you will need to transfer the design to your quilt top before layering with the backing and batting.

Use a sharp medium-lead or silver pencil, or mechanical pencil to mark the design. Test the pencil marks to guarantee that they will wash out of your quilt top when quilting is complete, or be sure your quilting stitches cover the pencil marks.

Manufactured quilting-design templates are available in many designs and sizes, and are cut out of a durable plastic template material that is easy to use.

To make a permanent quilting-design template, choose a template material on which to transfer the design. See-through plastic is the best because it will let you place the design while allowing you to see where it is in relation to your quilt design without moving it. Trace the design on the template material and either cut out the shape or just cut slits in the template material on the traced lines through which a pencil may be inserted.

Place the purchased or prepared template on the quilt top where you want it and trace around it with your marking tool. Pick up the quilting template and place again; repeat marking.

No matter what marking method you use, remember—the marked lines should never show on the finished quilt.

Preparing the Quilt Backing

In most cases, the materials list for each quilt in this book gives the size requirements for the backing, not the yardage needed. Exceptions to this are when the backing fabric is also used on the quilt top and yardage is given for both the top and backing in one amount.

A backing is generally cut at least 6" larger than the quilt top or 3" larger on all sides. For a 64" x 78" finished quilt, the backing would need to be at least 70" x 84".

To avoid having the seam down the center of the back, cut two fabric pieces the length of the backing needed; cut or tear one of these pieces in half, and sew half to each side of the second piece as shown in Figure 1.

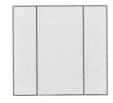
Figure 1

Figure 2

Quilt backings that are more than 88" wide may be pieced in horizontal pieces as shown in Figure 2.

Layering the Quilt Sandwich

If you will not be quilting on a frame, place the backing right side down on a clean floor or table. Start in the center and push any wrinkles or bunches flat. Use masking tape to tape the edges to the floor or table. The backing should be taut.

Center the batting on top of the backing; flatten out any wrinkles. Trim the batting to the same size as the backing. Fold the quilt top in half lengthwise and center on top of the batting, wrong side against the batting. Unfold quilt and, working from the center to the outside edges, smooth out any wrinkles or lumps.

To hold the quilt layers together for quilting, baste by hand or use safety pins. If basting by hand, thread a long thin needle with a long piece of unknotted white or off-white thread. Starting in the center, and leaving a long tail, make 4"–6"-long stitches toward the outside edge of the quilt top, smoothing as you baste. Start at the center again and work toward the outside as shown in Figure 3.

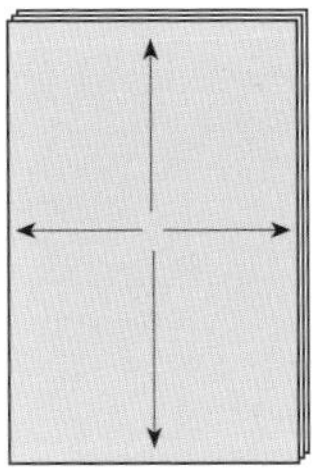

Figure 3

If quilting by machine, you may prefer to use safety pins to hold your fabric sandwich together. To use pins, start in the center of the quilt and pin to the outside, leaving pins open until all are placed. When you are satisfied that all layers are smooth, close the pins. To use basting spray, follow the manufacturer's instructions on the container.

Hand Quilting

Hand quilting is the process of placing stitches through the quilt top, batting and backing to hold them together. While it serves a functional purpose, it also adds beauty and loft to the finished quilt.

To begin, thread a sharp between needle with an 18" piece of quilting thread. Tie a small knot in the end of the thread. Position the needle about ½"–1" away from the starting point on the quilt top. Sink needle through the top into the batting layer but not through the backing. Pull the needle up at the starting point of the quilting design. Pull the needle and thread until the knot sinks through the top into the batting (Figure 4). Take small, even running stitches along the marked quilting line (Figure 5). Keep one hand positioned underneath to feel the needle go all the way through to the backing.

Figure 4   **Figure 5**

When you have nearly run out of thread, wind the thread around the needle several times to make a small knot and pull it close to the fabric. Insert the needle into the fabric on the quilting line and come out with the needle ½"–1" away, pulling the knot into the fabric layers the same as when you started. Pull and cut thread close to fabric. The end should disappear inside after cutting. Some quilters prefer to take a backstitch with a loop through it for a knot to end.

Machine Quilting

Prepare the quilt for machine quilting in the same way as for hand quilting. Use safety pins or basting spray to hold the layers together instead of basting with thread.

Presser-foot quilting is best used for straight-line quilting because the presser bar lever does not need to be continually lifted. Set the machine on a longer stitch length (3.0 or 8–10 stitches to the inch). Too tight a stitch causes puckering and fabric tucks, either on the quilt top or backing. An even-feed or walking foot

helps to eliminate the tucks and puckering by feeding the upper and lower layers through the machine evenly. Before you begin, loosen the amount of pressure on the presser foot.

For free-motion quilting, use your machine's darning foot with the feed dogs down. Refer to your sewing machine manual for other special instructions. Practice on a sample before trying this method on your quilt.

Making & Applying Straight-Grain Binding

To make double-fold, straight-grain binding, cut 2¼"-wide strips of fabric across the width or down the length of the fabric totaling the perimeter of the quilt plus 12". The strips are joined as shown in Figure 6; press seams open.

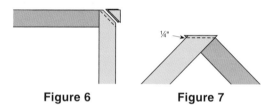

Figure 6   **Figure 7**

To make double-fold, bias-grain binding, cut 2¼"-wide bias strips from the binding-fabric yardage. Join the strips as shown in Figure 7 and press seams open.

Fold the joined binding strips in half with wrong sides together along the length, and press with no steam.

Lining up the raw edges, place the binding on the top of the quilt and begin sewing (again using the walking foot) approximately 6" from the beginning of the binding strip. Stop sewing ¼" from the first corner, leave the needle in the quilt, turn and sew diagonally to the corner as shown in Figure 8.

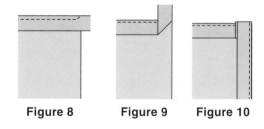

Figure 8   **Figure 9**   **Figure 10**

Fold the binding at a 45-degree angle up and away from the quilt as shown in Figure 9 and back down even with the raw edge of the next side of the quilt. Starting at the top raw edge of the quilt, begin sewing the next side as shown in Figure 10. Repeat at the next three corners.

As you approach the beginning of the binding strip, stop stitching and overlap the binding ends ½"; trim. Join the two ends with a ¼" seam allowance and press the seam open. Reposition the joined binding along the edge of the quilt and resume stitching to the beginning.

To finish, bring the folded edge of the binding over the raw edges and blind-stitch the binding in place over the machine-stitching line on the back side. Hand-miter the corners on the back as shown in Figure 11.

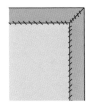

Figure 11

Making Continuous Bias Binding

Instead of cutting individual bias strips and sewing them together, you may make continuous bias binding.

Cut a square 18" x 18" from chosen binding fabric. Cut the square in half on one diagonal to make two triangles as shown in Figure 12. With right sides together, join the two triangles with a ¼" seam allowance as shown in Figure 13; press seam open to reduce bulk.

Figure 12   **Figure 13**

Mark lines every 2¼" on the wrong side of the fabric as shown in Figure 14. Bring the short ends right sides together, offsetting one line as shown in Figure 15; stitch to make a tube. This will seem awkward. Press seam open.

Figure 14   **Figure 15**

Begin cutting at point A as shown in Figure 16; continue cutting along marked line to make one continuous strip. Fold strip in half along length with wrong sides together; press. Sew to quilt edges as instructed previously for applying binding.

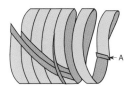

Figure 16

Adding Final Touches

If your quilt will be hung on the wall, a hanging sleeve, purchased plastic rings or fabric tabs are needed. The best choice for larger quilts is a fabric sleeve that will evenly distribute the weight of the quilt across the top edge, rather than at selected spots where tabs or rings are stitched, keep the quilt hanging straight and not damage the batting.

To make a sleeve, measure across the top of the finished quilt. Cut an 8"-wide piece of muslin equal to that length—you may need to join several muslin strips to make the required length.

Fold in ¼" on each end of the muslin strip and press. Fold again and stitch to hold. Fold the muslin strip with right sides together along the length. Sew along the long side to make a tube. Turn the tube right side out; press with seam at bottom or centered on the back.

Hand-stitch the top of the tube along the top of the quilt and the bottom of the tube to the quilt back, making sure the quilt lies flat. Stitches should not go through to the front of the quilt and don't need to be too close together. Slip a wooden dowel or long curtain rod through the sleeve to hang.

When the quilt is finally complete, it should be signed and dated. Use a permanent pen on the back of the quilt. Other methods include cross-stitching your name and date on the front or back or making a permanent label that may be stitched to the back. ❖

Special Thanks

We would like to thank the talented quilt designers whose
work is featured in this collection.

Betty Alderman
Buttons in My Cabin, 110

Lucy A. Fazely & Michael L. Burns
'Twas the Night Before Christmas, 141

Sue Harvey
Christmas Snow Globes, 121
Holly Wreath, 113

Sandra L. Hatch
Christmas Fun, 135
Christmas Stars Bed Topper, 132
Christmas Log Runner, 70
Holiday Stars Pillow, 102

Julie Higgins
Gingerbear Boys, 79

Connie Kauffman
Gift-Wrapped Toilet Seat Cover, 42
Holiday Towel Drapes, 27
Joy Snowman, 6
Sliding Penguins Apron, 50

Chris Malone
First Snow, 94
Flannel Fun Throw, 106
Flying Santas Tree Skirt, 15
Holly Jolly Ornaments, 32
Poinsettia Table Set, 67
Snowman Yo-Yo Lampshade
    Cover, 37

Rochelle Martin
Holiday Fun Candle Mat, 46

Linda Miller
Oh Christmas Tree, 155
Tree-mendous Ornaments, 169

Connie Rand
Christmas Kitty, 98
Waiting for Santa, 12

Jill Reber
Holly Party Set, 64

Judith Sandstrom
Gingerbread Patchwork, 118

Christine Schultz
Jolly Christmas Stocking, 20

Willow Ann Sirch
Christmas Rose Wreath, 129
Mad About Scraps Christmas Apron, 55
Poinsettia Holiday Card Holder, 40

Ruth Swasey
Christmas Snowballs, 138
Scrappy Red Christmas, 147

Rhonda Taylor
Surrounded by Flakes, 151

Jodi G. Warner
Holly Wreath Chair Jackets, 58

Julie Weaver
All Wrapped Up, 73
Christmas Squares, 76
Ho, Ho, Ho Wall Quilt, 87
Holly Jolly Snowmen, 124
Jolly Old St. Nick, 84

Fabric & Supplies

Page 6: Joy Snowman—white metallic, rayon and invisible thread from Sulky; WonderUnder fusible web from Pellon; and Dress It Up Tiny Snowflake buttons and Jingle All the Way Buttons from Jesse James & Co. Inc.

Page 12: Waiting for Santa—Star Machine Quilting Thread from Coats.

Page 15: Flying Santas Tree Skirt—Fabri-Tac fabric glue from Beacon Adhesives Inc., and HeatnBond fusible web from Therm O Web.

Page 46: Holiday Fun Candle Mat—Holiday Fun fabric collection from Benartex, and DMC pearl cotton.

Page 50: Sliding Penguins Apron—Hobbs Thermore batting, Steam-A-Seam2 fusible web from The Warm Co.; and metallic, rayon and invisible thread from Sulky.

Page 64: Holly Party Set—Master Piece 45 ruler and Static Stickers from Master Piece Products, and Presencia thread and pearl cotton.

Page 67: Poinsettia Table Set—Soft & Bright needled polyester batting from The Warm Co.

Page 70: Christmas Log Runner—December Day fabric collection by Thimbleberries for RJR Fabrics, Soft Touch cotton batting from Fairfield Processing, Star Machine Quilting Thread from Coats for piecing, 12-weight cotton thread from Sulky for quilting, and Quilt Basting Spray from Sullivans USA. Stitched on an Innovis 4000D sewing machine from Brother International; quilted on a Janome Memory Craft 6600 Professional Sewing & Quilting machine.

Page 73: All Wrapped Up—Warm & Natural cotton batting from The Warm Co., and Star Machine Quilting Thread from Coats.

Page 76: Christmas Squares—Warm & Natural cotton batting from The Warm Co., and Star Machine Quilting Thread from Coats.

Page 87: Ho, Ho, Ho Wall Quilt—Warm & Natural cotton batting from The Warm Co., and Star Machine Quilting Thread from Coats.

Page 98: Christmas Kitty—Star Machine Quilting Thread from Coats.

Page 102: Holiday Stars Pillow—Holiday Elegance fabric collection from RJR Fabrics, Cotton Classic cotton batting and pillow from Fairfield Processing Inc., and Star Machine Quilting Thread from Coats. Stitched on an Innovis 4000D sewing machine from Brother International.

Page 113: Holly Wreath—Peppermint & Holly Berries fabric collection by Nancy Halvorsen for Benartex, Star Machine Quilting Thread from Coats, Fairfield Machine 60/40 Blend batting, Appli-Kay Wonder from Floriani, 505 Spray and Fix from J.T. Trading, and Hill Creek Design buttons. Stitched on a Quilt Club 1000 Innovis sewing machine from Brother International.

Page 118: Gingerbread Patchwork—WonderUnder fusible web and Stitch-N-Tear fabric stabilizer from Pellon.

Page 121: Christmas Snow Globes—Christmas Treasures fabric collection by Susan Winget for

Benartex, Star Machine Quilting Thread from Coats, and Fairfield Machine 60/40 Blend batting used to make the sample project. Stitched on a Brother Innovis Quilt Club QC1000 sewing machine. Professionally machine-quilted by Sandy's Hide Away Quilts.

Page 124: Holly Jolly Snowmen—Lite Steam-A-Seam2 from The Warm Co., and Thermore batting from Hobbs.

Page 132: Christmas Stars Bed Topper—Winterlude fabric collection from Northcott, Soft Touch cotton batting from Mountain Mist, Star Machine Quilting Thread from Coats, and Quilt Basting Spray from Sullivans USA. Stitched on an Innovis 4000D sewing machine from Brother International.

Page 135: Christmas Fun—Holiday Helper fabric collection from Timeless Treasures, Soft Touch cotton batting from Mountain Mist, Star Machine Quilting Thread from Coats, and Quilt Basting Spray from Sullivans USA. Stitched on an Innovis 4000D sewing machine from Brother International.

Page 141: 'Twas the Night Before Christmas—Changing Season, Holiday Palette II, and Quilt Essential fabric collections from Classic Cotton Fabric Co.; Warm & Natural cotton batting from The Warm Co.; Dual Duty Plus all-purpose thread, clear nylon monofilament and Star Machine Quilting Thread from Coats; and Quilt Basting Spray from Sullivans USA.

Page 151: Surrounded by Flakes—Heirloom 100 percent cotton batting from Hobbs. Professionally machine-quilted by Sandy's Hide Away Quilts.